pasta sauces p 107 -109

Greens, Barley & Bea

Ch 8 => soup!

rice direction p 13 (w/no measuring
devices)

beans p. 129-130

wild rice p143

All' Amatriciana p. 172

Sausage pasta sauce p. 172

remove back bone from chick p.
174

FOOD FOR THOUGHT

By the same author

Bed and Board

An Offering of Uncles

The Supper of the Lamb

The Third Peacock

Hunting the Divine Fox

Exit 36

ROBERT FARRAR CAPON

FOOD FOR THOUGHT

Resurrecting the Art of Eating

HARCOURT BRACE JOVANOVICH
NEW YORK AND LONDON

Printed in the United States of America

Excerpts from the poetry of T. S. Eliot are reprinted by permission of Harcourt Brace Jovanovich, Inc. from his volume *Collected Poems 1909–1962;*
copyright, 1936, by Harcourt Brace Jovanovich, Inc.; copyright, 1943, 1963,
1964, by T. S. Eliot; copyright, 1971, by Esme Valerie Eliot.

Library of Congress Cataloging in Publication Data

Capon, Robert Farrar.
Food for thought.

Includes index.
1. Cookery.   I. Title.
TX715.C242   641.5   77-91475
ISBN 0-15-127267-0

First edition
B C D E

CONTENTS

FOOD FOR THOUGHT

INTRODUCTION

BEGINNING AT THE END

As I write this, I am living, temporarily, in an apartment complex that bills itself as a "prestige singles' community." I realize that the word "temporarily" tells you somewhat less, perhaps, than you'd like to know, but until I get both my nerve and your trust up to speed, let it pass. Besides, anyone who reaches the age of reason with even a single wit about him knows that, in a world where we tell time more with tears than with laughter, temporary quarters are pretty much the best we ever get. The wise man, right along with the fool, settles for whatever seizing of the day he can manage.

On the other hand, the phrase "prestige singles' community" tells you three full-fledged lies. What prestige there is resides solely in the mind of the PR man who wrote the copy for the ads. My apartment is located next to the town composting site, directly across from the sewage treatment sump for the entire complex. Indoors, things are not much more elegant: imperfectly spackled nail heads rust their way through the single coat of bargain paint; window catches, apparently designed to have a half-life of six months, have now, after three years, only one sixty-fourth of their catching power left; the drains are slow, except for the improperly vented one in the kitchen sink, which gurgles over its efficiency; birds fly through the heating ducts; and the walls are thin.

Let me refine that last a bit. The walls are not only thin; they are, ingeniously, selectively thin. As are the floors and ceilings. The only sound universally transmitted by these membranes is the noise of running water. I have concluded that the people who surround me are either very thirsty, very clean, very sick, or running a cottage industry washing out sausage casings for a wurst manufacturer.

All other sounds, however, are carried differentially by these several resonators. Anger, for example, seems to travel best horizontally. The stridencies of the people next door are as familiar to me as the sound of my own breathing—as is the furious bump of the hanger in the coat closet when he girds himself for yet another bout of leave-taking because, illogically but understandably, he might just as well go home if he's going to be hassled here too.

Ecstasy, on the other hand, rises from below. I presume that the pair just across the wall from me—the loud lady and the gentleman with a quick draw on the overcoat—do something other than fight. Given the ostensible nature of their arrangement, such a conclusion is inescapable. Yet for all I know, they could be playing whist in their occasional silences. No sigh, no whimper, no single tender word, come through the wall. But from downstairs! Every conceivable audible accompaniment of the tender passion comes straight up through the legs of my bed. Not to omit several inconceivable ones. Groans, yells, cries of joy and pain, and an assortment of thuds and crashes associable only with Flynn's Gym or a karate parlor are my nightly—no, that's too narrow—my constant background music. Except, inexplicably, between nine and eleven in the morning. Were it not for that small evidence that they are not inexhaustible—and for the frightening images their goings on produce in my mind—I would waste away with envy at the bravura of their sexual performance.

I do have my revenge, however. I play velocity exercises on the recorder at odd hours and make mistakes in the remote keys. More centrally to the purpose of this book, I make free and frequent use of three Chinese cleavers. Between the smashing of garlic and ginger and the production of my own chopped meat by hand, I am sure they think Thor has moved in upstairs to keep an eye on their proceedings. I would not lightly put the fear of God in anyone, but I am not above musing a little about the possibilities of coincidence between the thunder of my cooking and the lightning of their love.

Which brings us to the word "singles'." Little more need be said. As you have surmised, it is merely the bookkeeper's way of thinking about the inhabitants of the complex. The denizens themselves are resolutely at least double. If there are any hermits here, they are—to the point of total invisibility—true to their vocation.

Yet for all the pairing that gives the lie to the word "singles'," the biggest falsehood in the description is the use of the word "community." We nod to one another at the dumpster bin. That's about it. Oh, there's a pool, some tennis courts, an astroturf putting green, and a clubhouse with a bar and Cheezits. But the City, the Commonwealth—the Jerusalem for which we have longed and labored since we muffed our main chance in Eden—is pretty hard to see. Our *Res Publica* is a poor thing.

I meditate, sometimes, on the aptness of the word "complex." Examine the Latin roots. It comes from the verb *complecti,* to embrace, encircle, surround, comprehend. But who has thus embraced and comprehended us? God? Man? Some intelligent, caring being capable of forming a purpose, a vision of common life? No. Rather, a faceless complexor, a buck-chasing real-estate operation whose complexees we are, with all our private complexes and public complexities.

And the opposite of complex is simplex; of complexity, simplicity. But simple we are not, by a long shot. Under the veneer of oneness imposed by tennis court and club, we lead complicated lives. We sit by the pool in the backwash of a succession of attempts at union, none of which quite came off, but most of which are still somehow with us. It has made us a little—well, cautious. This is the land of the uncertain trumpet, where the wary wind their horns in pursuit of the diffident, where leisure suit and Farrah Fawcett-Majors look-alike stalk each other like porcupines making love.

And yet we stalk. For all the failure of community, I sense more hunting for the City here than almost anywhere —a more dogged chase, perhaps, than even angels give for that companionable state to which God draws all the divine beasts he has made. By default, no one has a *home* in this complex. If the places of our downsitting and uprising have even a hint of Jerusalem about them, it is because we have made them so. In the midst of the vagueness of our public life, we are explicit, even self-concious, about our domestic arrangements. True, our places seldom rise above the level of coziness, but they do often rise that far. And our personal conjunctions aim to rise considerably higher than that. We play a hard game of house here. We are in dead earnest about our domesticity. Ah, Dead Ernest. The fellow next door, coat in hand, caught like a stalled ox between two wives and two lives, trying to rise from the dead.

Is resurrection an odd category in a cookbook? Not really. One of the things Jesus did after the first Easter was whip up a breakfast of broiled fish. And besides, resurrection is the one essential category in human life. If we had a nice, neat life—if we had a simple, unified tissue of relationships on which an occasional shot of spot remover would do all that needs doing—why, then we would not be here. Old Dead Ernest could go home to his wife, say he was sorry, and roll over to sleep the sleep of the just. But we don't have lives here. Each of us has, instead, a death—a collection of former lives whose soul, whose unifying, life-giving principle, has, alas, gone galley west and left us stalled, too.

And if you think about that, even a little, I have a suspicion you will not find it so odd. We may be distinctive here, but I don't think we're all that different. We are a kind of sacrament, a notable sign, of what is true, in some sense, everywhere. There are mortgages out on you too, probably. And if they were all called in at once . . . ?

But not to make you gloomy. This is a bit weighty before lunch. The category is resurrection, not death; the freedom of life, not the bondage of the grave. The only thing you have to do with death is to admit it, to stop pretending to a life you don't have, and to open yourself to the power of someone else's gift of a new life. That's not an evangelistic pitch, by the way, though it could be. If you like, take it simply at the lowest, truest level: we need friends of extraordinary stature. Not ones who can put up with the odd fault here or there, but ones who can raise the dead, who can, on their own, accept the unacceptable by moving in on us with a wholly new life—who can free us from the curse of having to argue a hopeless case. I think I have a couple of those. At least, I find myself less often constrained to plead my own cause; so that's evidence of something. I'm not so sure about Ernest next door, though. I feel like cooking. He seems only to feel cooked.

Wish him well though. And her, too. May they both have the grace to raise each other—and to shut up and take the resurrection when it's offered. Amen. Meanwhile, you and I have life to enjoy. Remember the breakfast of broiled fish. If the promises of the Gospel are any good at all, we should do considerably better than that.

Shelter Island, N.Y.
October 1977

I

LUNCH AND HISTORY

Let me take two boned chicken breasts out of the freezer before we begin. Lunch will be chicken and asparagus over rice; dessert, a Hershey bar with almonds. Somebody cleaned me out of beer, but there's the better part of a jug of California Rhine wine, so all is not lost.

I hope you will not mistake this for an excessively relaxed beginning; my first paragraph, in fact, is positively intense. In three short sentences, I have given you an index to no fewer than twelve of the major subjects of this book.

1. CHICKEN:
At forty-nine cents a pound, it's the ultimate bargain in meat.

2. ECONOMY:
Only whole chickens are that cheap. Cut up your own, save from ten cents to a dollar fifty a pound, get twelve servings from two birds—plus soup, fat, and chicken salad in the bargain.

3. BONING:
I shall teach you how to do it. Why pay the supermarket for cutting things up wrong?

4. FREEZER:
One of the few instances of mechanical progress that represents unqualified forward motion. As long as the Lighting

Company doesn't succumb to a hurricane, it's the best servant in the house. If you use it right, it pays for itself (or for the refrigerator in which it lives) in less than a year.

5. TWO BREASTS:

Unless you're feeding a battalion, freeze things in small and separable quantities.

6. LUNCH:

An important, not an unimportant, meal. As a matter of fact, there are no unimportant meals, only people with insufficient self-esteem to bother cooking estimably.

7. ASPARAGUS:

And Vegetables in general. When they are fresh and in season, eat them; when not, use items that were canned or frozen when they were. Corollary: Always use canned tomatoes, except in August and September.

8. RICE:

And Grains in general. And Pasta in particular. And, by extension, Beans.

9. NUTRITION:

Rice and Beans. Hoppin' John. Pasta e Fagioli. The human race discovered most of the home truths about nourishment before the nutritionists bored everyone silly. Corollary: Any school of cookery more than two hundred years old is sound; cuisines with less than fifty years under their belt need watching.

10. DESSERT:

I give you blanket permission. If you will just stop eating between meals, you can eat sweets to your stomach's content—which occurs sooner at the end of a meal than at three in the afternoon—and to your heart's content too, as you will manufacture less lard to lug around your middle.

11. BEER:

A maligned beverage, for all its popularity. Some foods do not go with wine. There is nothing that cannot be washed down with beer. Corollary (with the Surgeon General's warning): The same is true of Scotch, cognac, Calvados, marc, grappa, and Chinese firewater. But rise frequently from the table to see if your legs are still working—and don't expect to feel good in the morning.

12. WINE:

The perfect beverage, but one presently in danger of being rendered problematical by a motley army of snobs, popularizers, and speculators. This has long been true of $Wine_1$, or French Wine; it is, alas, rapidly becoming true of $Wine_2$, California.

And that's only one paragraph. I suggest we press on.

The chicken breasts have not thawed as much as they might, but if you'll hand me my Chinese cleaver, we can begin to get things ready anyway. We will use 3/8-inch cubes of meat, so all that needs to be done is to cut them into three strips lengthwise and then crosswise into as many pieces as necessary. Watch: both hands on top of the cleaver —then simply bear down hard with all your weight and rock the blade a little as you go. There. Done. You finish.

This dish is Chinese, so the pieces of meat get a little marinade to sit in before cooking. Just throw together in a bowl a teaspoon of light soy sauce, a tablespoon of sake, a splash of peanut oil, and a turn or two of black pepper. Stir it up, chicken and all, cover the bowl with a plate, and slide it to the back of the counter.

After that, you can fix the rice. One cup of the long-grain white should do us. Now, just wash it eleven times . . .

Dear me. I detect an ever so slight narrowing of your mind's eye. Being lectured on domesticity in dead earnest by someone living in a singles' complex is bad enough, but this is a bit much. Why *white* rice? Why not brown for better nutrition? Why wash it? Why flush what little goodness it has left down the sink? And why, above all, *eleven* times? What are we into? Numerology?

I respect your sentiments but, for the moment, I'm

afraid I shall have to be firm with you. It is, after all, my lunch. The philosophical underpinnings will come later. Right now, suffice it to say that the rice is white because I always serve white rice with this dish; it is washed so it won't be a sticky mass after it's cooked; and it's washed eleven times . . . Well, I have found that eleven changes of water is usually enough. Nothing sacred. It's simply that if you're going to wash rice at all, you really wash it. So just take the pot of rice in one hand and the sieve in the other, fill the pot with cold water, pour it off into the sieve, knock the rice back into the pot—and don't lose count until you're sure you're over eleven. Meanwhile I'll cut up the asparagus.

Notice, by the way, the method of cutting. First, you break each spear in two by holding it at the ends and bending it till it snaps at some appropriately tender point. When you've done them all, you throw the bottom parts in a plastic bag and put them away in the freezer for a future asparagus soup. Then you take the top halves and cut them, diagonally, into ⅜-inch pieces. If you like, the very tips of the spears can be left larger. This is a *kow,* or chunk-cut, dish: All the ingredients in the finished presentation have similar shapes, to please the eye as well as the palate.

If you find that a bit high church, I hope you will at least be patient with me. For one thing, shape does make a difference: the same sauce served over spaghetti, on the one hand, or ziti, on the other, makes two quite distinct dishes. For another, I have spared you the ultimate in popery-jiggery. Left to my own devices, I would use what is called the rolling diagonal cut: the knife not only enters the spear on the bias; the spear itself is rolled toward you as you cut, giving the resultant chunk a faceted look.

In any case, all we have to do now is put the cut-up asparagus in another bowl, rinse it a few times, and leave it covered with cold water to keep it fresh. After that, we smash two large cloves of garlic to a pulp, wash the salt off two tablespoons Chinese black beans (rather forbidding-smelling things, but only when they're uncooked), and mince them a bit. Then we cook the rice.

You may, of course, do that by adding a shy two cups water for every cup raw rice (no salt, please), covering the pot (a nice heavyweight one, large enough to hold triple the volume of rice and water), and bringing it to a fast boil. You then remove the cover and let the water boil away till it starts to disappear down the little holes which have formed in the rice. After that, put the cover back, turn the heat down as low as you can get it, and let the rice steam for twenty minutes. Fluff it up with a fork, turn off the heat, and let it sit (covered, of course) till you need it.

There is, however, a more excellent way I'd like to show you. Or at any rate, a more excellent refinement of the basic method I just gave you. Instead of measuring rice and water with cups, you give them a personal touch. Using the hollow of your hand you measure out a palmful of rice for every person to be served. Add an extra palmful for the sake of safety and generosity, and wash as before. Then put the rice in the pot and add cold water till it comes to just below the first knuckle when your fingertip is barely resting on the top of the rice.

In fact, this works out to something like seven eighths of an inch, give or take a little (old rice should have a bit more water), but the trick is to learn to read your own personal depth gauge. After all, you will presumably be able to count more dependably on having a hand than on having cups or rulers. And besides, it makes it more your rice that way. You may even happen to have a conveniently located scar on your left middle finger which will introduce some possibly colorful personal history into your cooking. In any case, you have a knuckle, so you're home free; cook as above.

Once again, however, I think I detect the beginnings of a mental reservation on your part. It's not simply that this

rice directions

may be rather more fuss than you're used to when it comes to lunch. Perhaps it isn't. Perhaps you're a kindred soul, and the two of us could go on forever pleasing ourselves with midday delights. What troubles you more deeply, I think, is that this whole exercise, with its attention to water depths and rolling diagonal cuts, may be an anachronism in this the first quarter of our third American century. Going through all this ritual at eleven on a weekday morning is indeed playing house, but in a way that no one seems to play it any more. The most recently dead Ernest who actually lived this way probably chunked his last chicken sometime before World War II.

"After all," you say to me, "isn't housekeeping in general, and home cooking in particular, on the decline? Wasn't there recently a set of figures in the papers which pointed out that, whereas ten years ago one food dollar out of five was spent on eating out, we now spend one out of three? And didn't the article say that, according to the restaurant and fast-food industry, the figure will be one out of two a decade hence? The supermarket moguls are not happy. The wave of the future seems mostly fish and chips; what they see on its crest is not fresh meat and produce for home cooking, but burger wrappers and thick-shake cups."

Well, I'll give you that, if you like. There's no use arguing with statistics—though it's worth noting that the dire ten-year projection comes, obviously, from food industry types with dollar signs for eyes. My point is not that everyone actually goes to these lengths to get a noonday meal. It is not even that everyone should. It is simply that if this kind of house-playing were to disappear completely, human nature as the race has come to know and love it would have a hard time surviving. I don't really care about the statistics. All they prove is what people actually do. What I'm concerned about is the false assumption that what people actually do can safely be taken as an index of what they ought to do.

I apologize for dragging in such old-fashioned expressions as "human nature" and "ought," but then, if my way of cutting up asparagus is not about to take the nation by storm, why should I worry about whether my philosophical vocabulary can win a popularity contest? It's simply that I refuse to work without a concept of human nature from which I can derive some notion of what might be better or worse for me. And I even more resolutely refuse to let some statistician snowball me into accepting a trend for a concept. Human beings, thanks to their possession of reason and freedom, can think or do any damn fool thing they want. In fact, they regularly do so. But to take the results of that foolishness and extrapolate them into a philosophy! Worse yet, to think that when you have done that, you have done something intellectually respectable . . .

The trouble, you see, is that we have lost sight of the meaning of the word "natural." We think that, just as long as no one is forcibly interfering with a process, whatever happens will be in accord with the natures of the beings involved. Now, while that may be true if you're thinking of ants, alligators, or asteroids—of things whose natures are more or less self-achieving—it's not true of human beings. If they want to be what they are, they have to choose to be it; because with no outside pressure at all, they can easily choose to be something else. Quite often unknowingly. They can be doing, as they see it, only "what comes naturally"; but in that very process, they can gum up their real nature.

You do not believe me? Consider the following random observations.

1. A long stick has two ends. Even a small child has enough of a grip on human nature, reason, and freedom to take in that fact and to see the operational consequences of it. Yet all children invariably choose to watch only the end that interests them—the end, say, with which they flick the cat's tail. The other end—the one that knocks the crystal compote off the coffee table—seems always to surprise them with its existence.

2. Most adults have a whole collection of psychodynamic

long sticks. Some show home movies and are astonished when their guests fall asleep. Others spend lifetimes complaining about injuries sustained as a result of leading with the chin. A few even profess surprise that their anger makes other people mad.

3. Man invented the automobile because his nature is such that he likes to get where he is going (*a*) quickly, (*b*) safely, and (*c*) economically. He failed to note, however, that the other end of the stick was labeled Detroit. What he actually got, therefore, not only cancelled out *a*, *b*, and *c* but also effectively destroyed half the places formerly worth going to.

4. Human beings eat food either because it tastes good or because it satisfies their bodily needs. Accordingly, we should expect that, given a choice, man will prefer wine to soda pop and bread to quilt stuffing. That, however, is not quite how it works out. Witness the pullman loaf, for openers—with a fast-food taco for the main course and a takeout frosted for dessert.

The argument, therefore, that human nature is as human beings do, is flawed. Our real needs and exigencies go right on, even though our actual performances fail to meet them. That people eat more takeout food than they used to; that what they eat tastes less like food every year; that in two decades, alas not *per impossible,* America will have turned into one giant fast-food operation; even that, God forbid, there soon will not be one domestic cook among us capable of a decent tripe in red sauce; all of that proves nothing. Or better said, it proves only that we will have used the gift of our nature to beat our humanity insensible to its real needs.

But just as the argument is negligible, so is my prophecy of doom. Human nature, for all its faults, isn't going to go away. Even in that dull new world, where nobody cooks for himself—and where house, like euchre, is a game no one plays any more—what is really natural to us will be waiting to jump

out and scare us back to our senses. Some brave soul will always be found to do the job. Even if he has, idiotically, to fall
in love with tripe by reading about it in a cookbook from a
garage sale—even if he has to scour the land to find a pet-food
manufacturer who will indulge his madness and sell him a
couple of beef paunches rather than grind them all into the
K-9 Kwisine—he will do it. And one fine day, after long
darkness, his family will sit down to Tripe Niçoise and rise
up conquering and to conquer. The perennial revolution in
the name of taste will have begun again.

You do not think so? Let me suggest two lines of argument: one to prove that, by the very nature of humanity, the
odd but necessary soul will always be found; and the other to
suggest that oddly enough, in the midst of the general ship-
wreck of cookery, there are probably now more such types
awaiting discovery than ever before. You see, I hope, that
I not only suspect the best of you; I also think you have
plenty of company.

To grasp the first proposition, you need to note that
people often misconstrue what we mean when we say that
all men possess human nature. They let legal or even theological considerations of equality lull them into assuming
that everyone possesses all the attributes of human nature in
the same degree. They forget that humanity is a social as
well as an individual notion, that no one of us can ever hold
the fullness of human nature in himself alone, and that, frequently, others will have to supply for us those aspects of
our nature which we lack.

For example, consider the usual definition: Man is a
rational animal. That's true, of course, of every creature
born of woman. But it doesn't stop some of the children of
Eve from being less rational or more animal than others.
There are people who wouldn't recognize a line of reasoning even if it offered them a free lunch; there are others who
make love as if they were logs. But we bear our nature socially as well as individually. The gentleman with the chronic

risibilis, risibilis, risibile ⇒
laughab?
amusing
funny
or
that
can
laugh

FOOD FOR THOUGHT   18

inability to recognize a good deal may well be blessed by the
company of a lady who hasn't missed an offer in her life; the
woman with the vegetable approach to sex may find a lover
who will surprise her with her unrealized animality.

And that's from just the *essential* definition of humanity.
If you take some *accidental* definitions, it becomes even
clearer that help is always on the way—that some of us will
always undertake the job of sacramentalizing what others
can't express. Consider the old textbook example of definition *per accidens,* for instance: Every man is capable of
laughter, *omnis homo risibile* as they used to say when
Latin wasn't the unfunny subject it is now.

Let us suppose that you have spent the better part of an
evening with sociologists or educational psychologists. It
will be quite clear to you by eleven that risibility is not
evenly distributed among the members of the race. As the
night wears on, you may well find yourself—even to the point
of proctologist stories or parrot jokes—desperately trying to
sacramentalize for them the sense of humor they have buried
under a mountain of jargon. I myself find limericks handy
in such straits. When I break into a discussion of, say, socio-
metric analysis with "There was a young man from Berlin"
or "There once was a Turkish cadet," I do it to offer myself
as a living sacrament, a real presence of the fact that measurement, like everything else about us, is fundamentally hilarious. One's reward for such kindness may, of course, be an
answering deluge of shaggy dog stories. But that's all right.
In the exchanges of the City of our common nature, we bear
one another's burdens too.

More to the point, though, is another accidental definition: Man is the animal who cooks his food, *omnis homo
coquus.* Need I say more? Breathes there a man with soul so
dead, who never to himself has said, "Let's invite them before they invite us"? Have you not willingly ministered taste
to the untasting rather than run the risk of being ministered
to by them? And have you not, when you weren't quick

Coquus - cook - noun

enough with the invitation, borne heroically one or more of
the following outrages? Vulcanized flank steak? Barbecued
chicken with raw second joints? Lasagne with canned tomato
soup? Sole Mornay with Cheez-Whiz? Homemade strawberry
shortcake with nondairy whipped topping? Marshmallow
sweet potatoes? Candlestick salad? (This last, a kiddy cookbook specialty featuring a perpendicular banana, is perhaps
the ultimate obscenity in fruit salads. With an imaginative
garnish, it could be turned into the quintessential culinary
joke, but adults who serve it seem always to lack the necessary inventiveness.)

On, then, to the second line of argument—to the proposition that you and I are not alone in this battle for human
nature, that the time is ripe for a whole army of likeminded
souls to join us in a new crusade.

As I see it, those who play house with any degree of
seriousness at all (and that's most of the population) can
be divided into three groups: those starting out at the game;
those who, for whatever reason, find themselves forced to
start over; and those who, even with no dramatically new
circumstances in their lives, are ready for a fresh start at
cookery. If someone is not in the first two groups, he is,
though perhaps unknowingly, bound to be in the third. In
any case, he and you and I are part of a large crowd, and
this book is meant to give us hope.

Take those just starting out at cookery, for example.
I'm not thinking of teenagers in their mothers' kitchens making their first pass at béarnaise sauce. They're not really playing house yet, just playing at it. I'm thinking of them when
they're out for the first time running their own show, alone
or with others: the newly emancipated, the newly wed, or
the newly allied, whichever the case may be.

They start out with a clean slate, as it were, with a
situation in which the bones of housekeeping and cookery
have not yet been covered with baby fat. I shall have rather
a lot to say to them—and they to us. I'm a great believer in

the pictures taken of day-old babies. If you know how to read them, you can see, more clearly than you will be able to for years, the man or woman to come. So too with day-old houseplayers. If they pay good attention to the bone structure of what they're up to, they'll be able to see better than almost anybody the reality we're all about.

The person who lives alone for the first time, for example, is confronted instantly with the necessity of developing a healthy self-esteem. He needs to discipline himself, to develop a settled habit of thinking kindly of his own company. And for that, there is no better exercise than paying himself the compliment of regular, decently cooked meals, eaten seated at a table, with a glass of wine and enough quiet time to think or read or dream. How sad, therefore, when the lives of people in such a potentially rich state are spent in a frantic run for company, fueled only by double-crispy chicken and flaked and formed beef. If we are not fit for solitude, we will never be anything but dangerous in company. How nice to learn that early.

Again, if the first-timer happens to be starting out with others (one or more), the situation is even fuller of chances to begin at the true beginning. Another human being in the house makes it the City indeed, and all the courtesies of the City need to be invoked forthwith. Love may bring them together, but love is never enough—or at least, it can never rest content short of that honoring and cherishing of each other which keeps the City from turning into Babel, or the Bottomless Pit.

And for that long course in mutual esteem, what better classroom than kitchen and table? Bed has its contributions, of course, but it's across the Board that we are perpetually invited into dialogue. How sad, then, when sour silences brood over TV dinners, and when peanut butter is the only real food in the house. Cookery calls for discipline, to be sure; but if it can be done at all, it must. Few other things lie as close, for good or ill, to the working center of our nature.

On the other hand, take the second group: those who are starting housekeeping over. They have other lessons to learn and teach. The reasons for their new beginning may be as various as the mind of man, or the changes and chances of this mortal life can make them—widowhood, divorce, re-marriage, retirement, or just a move from large quarters to small. But the challenge is always the same: how to begin again without either denying the past or becoming its slave. T. S. Eliot put it neatly: "History may be servitude, / His-tory may be freedom." But the choice is always up to us. There is, in every life, a time for moving on that comes only when you have gotten comfortable with the idea of not hav-ing to move at all; and it comes, usually, rather late than soon. Eliot again:

> Old men ought to be explorers
> Here and there does not matter
> We must be still and still moving
>   . . .
> . . . In my end is my beginning.

What's that got to do with cooking? Well, if you have to ask, you've never changed kitchens. Setting up a new one is the best and clearest of all the diagrams of how history is to be handled. To begin with, there is no point, and no way, of cutting yourself off from your past: nobody begins to cook anew—or to live again—from scratch. But second, there is no point and no way of starting over as before: the past must be sorted, classified, and culled with high serious-ness. The first effort, therefore, must always be to recapture the sense of being on a pilgrimage, the resolve to travel light. After that, a simple Junk/Baggage classification, made with ruthless honesty, will do the rest.

Let me give you a sample worksheet to illustrate the principles involved.

As you can see, Ernest has some odd priorities, and he hasn't worked nearly long enough on his list; but at least

TRAVELIGHT MOVERS AND COUNSELORS

KITCHEN/DINING ROOM PACKING LIST

Name: **ERNEST**   OLD   DEAD
     last   first   middle

Destination: 1001 SINGLES' COMPLEX DRIVE

JUNK
(Do not pack at all)

(a) *Useless Junk:*
Electric can opener. Hollow stem champagne glasses. Iced tea spoons. Electric knife, wedding present stemware. Cat food. canned taco sauce. Salt mill.

(b) *Dangerous Junk:*
Japanese combination kitchen saw and bread knife. snack crackers. Habit of eating between meals without conversing. Drinking between meals. Habit of cooking to avoid conversation. Hard liquor.

BAGGAGE
(Pack as directed)

(a) *Excess Baggage (Pack only on last trip):*
Cats, wine cellar (sad!) Dining room furniture. Good stemware (but try for 1/2 doz.) Cookbook collection. Food processor.

(b) *Desirable Baggage (Pack, if possible):*
Electric blender. Chinese steamer. Electric mixer/grinder. Egg beater. Toaster. Cheese grater. Nutmeg grater. 25 lb. bag rice. Plum sauce. 1/2 doz. 16 oz. claret glasses. Plastic containers. Plastic wrap. Freezer paper. Tape.

(c) *Necessary Baggage (Pack first):*
Wok. chopsticks. Chinese cleavers. Sharpening stone and steel. Cutting board. Cookbooks: Pellaprat, Fannie Farmer (old ed.) Chinese, Italian, Swedish. 12 qt. pot. 3 other pots. Iron frying pan + dutch oven. Bowls. wooden spoons, whisk. Mortar and pestle. Spices/herbs. Red pepper sauce. Sesame oil. Hoisin, brown bean sauce. chili paste. ginger. Salted turnip. star anise. Lt. and dark soy. Oyster sauce, Black beans. Pepper mill. Plates. Glasses. Jars.

it's an indication. The main trick, once the list is made, is to select items for packing from the bottom up—and to stop packing as far from the top as possible. This book is especially for him. Once he seriously tries to take none of his history with him unthinkingly, he will find how well his history has equipped him to make a resourceful new beginning. He is, obviously, a man of some parts; but he has to put most of them down before he'll be able to put all of them together.

The last of the three groups—those who are ready for a new beginning—is perhaps the most interesting. Its members have all the advantages and drawbacks of the first two, plus some other peculiar to themselves. With the newly wed or the newly established, they share, presumably, the virtue of enthusiasm over the present arrangement of their lives. In addition, they have, like Ernest, a considerable, even estimable, experience to draw on. Unlike him, however, they can essay their new beginning at leisure and in peace; if they have mastered the courtesies of the City to the extent their stability purports, there will be none of his attendant *Sturm und Drang* while they try to refresh their grip on domesticity.

They will, nonetheless, have their problems. It is the very ease with which they have so far accepted the pattern of their lives that will give them the most trouble. After all, unless they hold monthly yard sales, their history is just going to hang around. The uncriticized agglomeration of things and habits—the cat food and the cats, the canned taco sauce and the electric knife, the snack crackers and the four-martini cocktail hour—that over the years have moved in on them and defined a lifestyle is not about to be absent (as it is with newlyweds) or wrenched from their hands (cf. Ernest).

Members of the third group must, therefore, avoid two extremes. On the one hand, they must not think that their old patterns can go on unbroken save for a few minor alterations; on the other, they must not pretend they can chuck it all and start fresh. They must do the job where and as they are, but they must really do a job of it.

An illustration? Behold the blue crab, genus *Callinectes*, the beautiful swimmer. He grows by shedding his shell—and, by divine providence, he graces man's table as the soft-shelled crab. But have you ever thought what that means to the crab? I don't mean ending up on your table. In the Peaceable Kingdom we shall simply thank each other for such courtesies and get on with the party on the Holy Mountain, where no one hurts or destroys. Rather, I have in mind what it means to the crab to have to grow that way. Physically, man is lucky. He has his skeleton on the inside, and, obligingly enough, it grows right along with him with nary a thought required. But socially, man is very much like the crab. His relationships are like exoskeletons and, like the crab's shell, they harden. If man is to continue to grow, he must continually break out of relational shells, discard them, and let new ones form.

Now for the first two groups, this is easy. In fact, it is practically inevitable. A little scary perhaps, but at least expected, and often desired. But for the third group it can only feel, well, unnatural, even though it is the course of nature itself. Their very acceptance of their shells leads them to dread the vulnerability they know they will feel without them. And yet, for them, as for everybody, shedding the shell remains the only way to grow. No one, not even the crab, can go back to the beginning; we can only start again where we are by laying aside the no longer useful carapace. This book, therefore, is most especially for them; for they, perhaps more than all the rest, need a new beginning.

Lunch, however, is still before us, and things must not be allowed to degenerate into gravity at midday. Pour us some wine then, and I shall get on with the cooking. As a matter of fact, with minor variations, the dish I am about to make can be turned into soft-shelled crab with black bean sauce.

II

DUE SEASONING

**T**he rice, I think, will still be nearly hot enough, so all we need to do is give it a little low heat while I cook the dish. Just let me put the ring for the wok on the stove and set the wok in it. Then we're ready to go.

There are people who teach Chinese cooking classes who tell you not to bother with the ring because, they say, it puts the wok too far above the flame. But that's a ridiculous solution to the problem. The wok, with its round bottom, wobbles every which way on the burner grid. What they should teach you is how to find, or make, a lower ring. Chinese stir-frying, with its requisite slap and dash, calls for a firm foundation. Cooking in an unsupported wok is like trying to do fine cabinet work on a card table. To a cook of any competence at all, it's a form of Chinese torture.

But with that prejudice out of my system, we're set. Pour the water off the asparagus, set it, the bowl of chicken, and the saucer of garlic and black beans somewhere on the stove, and put about eight of those frozen chicken-stock cubes in a little pot on the fire to melt. Now then: sake bottle and peanut oil at the ready; *siou hok* in the left hand, *wok chan* in the right . . .

Oh! We forgot the cornstarch. The liquid in the dish gets thickened at the end. Take one of those N.Y. Mets gas-station glasses, put in two tablespoons cornstarch and dissolve it in some cold water. A mixture with the consistency of light cream will do nicely. Meanwhile, back at the wok . . .

What's a *siou hok* and a *wok chan?* Well, basically, a ladle and a pancake turner designed for use in a round-bottomed pan. Lacking Chinese hardware altogether, you can prepare this dish in an ordinary iron Dutch oven or frying pan, but the proper Chinese equipment won't give you such a hard time. Working with substitutes is like trying to rip a board with a crosscut saw: it can be done, but the tool feels as if it's dragging its feet.

Off we go then: fire turned up high under the wok; a little peanut oil poured in the *siou hok* and swirled into the wok with a circular motion so it coats the pan as it slides toward the bottom. Add a pinch of salt, wait a bit till it just begins to smoke, and flick the garlic and black beans into the wok with the *wok chan*. Keep it all moving until the garlic just starts to brown and a nice pungency rises up to meet you (five to ten seconds, not much more) ; then toss in the asparagus and stir-fry (using both tools with vigor, turning the chunks over and over) for about forty seconds; add a generous *siou-hok*ful of chicken stock (more if you want more sauce, but don't drown it) , boil, cover for another minute or so, then empty the wok into the serving dish. (The best way to do this is to turn the fire off, shovel the ingredients into the ladle with the turner and empty the ladle into the dish, repeating the performance until the wok is empty, juice and all.)

Next, the chicken: fire on again, another swirl of peanut oil in the wok, a little salt, and then the chunks of chicken— all stir-fried slapdash until the meat turns white (thirty seconds, perhaps; at any rate, keep it moving so nothing browns at all.)

Finally, empty the serving dish back into the wok (you note, I hope, that you now have one heated serving dish ready for the final presentation) , bring it all to a boil and, using a tablespoon, stir in enough cornstarch and water solution to thicken it to your liking—well short, however, of the bad-Chinese-restaurant jellied-glop stage. Mix well and empty into the serving dish once again. We're ready to eat. Just take the rice to the table in the pot while I chop up the scallions I forgot—I always like a sprinkling on top for color and flavor.

There. *Bon appetit,* or whatever they say in China. Oriental languages are not my specialty. How about the shortest Latin grace of all [*Benedictus benedicat*] *Amen.*

↳ blessed ↠ he blesses may the blessed one bls.

Ah! Lovely.

Some idiot once made a rule that a man could praise his own wine but not his own cooking. That way lies madness—and the practical certainty of wretched food. I like a cook who smiles out loud when he tastes his own work. Let God worry about your modesty; I want to see your enthusiasm.

You agree, that's a perfect lunch? Light, but with enough taste to make you know you've eaten something. And nothing overpowered: the chicken tastes like chicken, the asparagus, like asparagus, and the sauce tastes like everything put together—which is a third taste in itself. All that pleasure, plus balanced nourishment.

With that under our belts, however, we're ready for the first actual step in your new beginning at cookery: the refreshing, by way of a drastic pruning, of your approach to seasoning.

Why do I begin there? And why by pruning? On the one hand, you are accustomed to thinking of seasonings as things superimposed upon food, usually somewhere near the end of the cooking process; on the other, you are surprised that I suggest cutting back, for I am obviously a devotee of anything that will enhance and enliven taste.

Let me reassure you. The word "pruning" is used neither unadvisedly nor lightly. Trees are pruned in order that, with suckers and ill-grown branches removed, they might bear more fruit; I intend for you to flower mightily after this exercise in austerity. Your cooking will be redolent of tarragon, saffron, cardamom, and dill, of parsley, sage, rosemary, and the rest. But only after we lop most of them off the shelf for a while. And as for putting the subject of seasoning first . . . Well, that calls for a little metaphysical excursion.

I grant you that the logical order of subjects in cookery (and, certainly, the one adopted by most authors of cookbooks) runs something like: Equipment, Materials, Methods, Seasonings. But not every logical starting point is a true beginning. What we're looking for is not just an opener but a *principium*, an *archē*—a beginning in the full sense of the word: a first, essential principle within which the goal of what we are up to is implicit from the outset. Indeed, what we want is a *terminus a quo*, which is actually a sacrament, a very present *praegustatum* of that ultimate Taste, which is our end. → Starting point

And if that's what we want, then seasoning must come first. Man, as we've said, is the animal who cooks his food. But cooking isn't just heating things up, just as architecture isn't simply the piling of blocks one on top of another. Cooking is the expansion, by reason and skill, of flavor into art. All distinctively human activity involves a kind of priestly lifting of nature into forms that, while new to nature itself, are actually elations and perfections of it. Dogs like taste well enough; but what man has done with garlic!

Enough of that, however. There is something even more important behind and within taste. God, if we believe the Scriptures, created the world out of delight; and he runs it, not by shoving things around with main force, but by attraction—by desire for Himself as the Highest Good.

You thought the world was run by physical laws? Dear me! Reformulate that for yourself immediately, because it is a classical instance of the reductionist fallacy. Physical laws don't *do* anything—and they explain things only at the lowest level. They are simply descriptions of how desire for the good works out in practice. An example: Everything Arthur Schnabel does when he plays, say, the *Emperor Concerto* can be described physically; but if you want to talk strictly—at the level of ultimate explanation—you have to say he plays it out of a desire to make music. Likewise, all cooking is physical activity; but the cook is drawn, throughout the process, by the good of taste.

Seasoning, therefore, is a sacrament, a real presence in a specific matter, of the desire for the Highest Good. Man, when he sprinkles his oregano, is doing in his uniquely human way what the stars in their courses do in their own: moving, in response to delight, toward Delight Himself—and making the process delightful every step of the way. It is desire that transforms mere existence into life; accordingly, seasoning is the true beginning of the subject of cookery. Q.E.D.

To illustrate the proof, take a severely limited example. Imagine yourself in the hospital for a long stay, confined, perhaps, in a body cast. However, the worst—the pain, with its nagging but real ability to keep you at least morbidly interested in your life—is over. You are now up to your counterpane in the boredom of recuperation: you exist, if that is not too strong a word, in a narrow and tiresome space with interminable and undifferentiated time on your hands. What is it that transforms these dismal parameters of your life into high time and desirable place? What is it that makes you feel like *living?* Well, apart from a few welcome visitors, isn't it the prospect, followed by the fact, of three meals a day? With nothing left to you but the meager sacrament of a diet of hospital food, your roots are sent rain, because it provides you with nothing less than a real presence of that Desire by which the Lifegiving Spirit—the *Dominus Vivificans*—draws you *ex nihilo* into being, and out of mere being into Life.

But I promised you simplification, and here I am with the Latin shaker, sprinkling theological oregano over everything. *Eheu!*

Before we pursue the analysis of seasoning into specifics, however, let me make clear what I mean by the subject: as I understand it, seasoning comprises everything in cookery except the basic raw materials themselves—and even many of the raw materials can become seasonings when added to other things. For example, a cut of crossrib of beef, nicely tied for pot-roasting, is not a seasoning; but everything else in the final dish is: the olive oil in which it is browned; the chopped onion and garlic tossed into the pot after browning to capture color and add flavor; the thyme, and marjoram, and the savory; the single bay leaf and the solitary clove; the end of the bottle of California Burgundy to rinse the pot after the onions and garlic; the pinch of sugar to take the curse off the wine; the parsley, the pepper, and the salt; and finally—because it is every bit as much a seasoning, bringing things to ripeness and perfectness of age, as all the rest—the discreet quantity of water that makes the many into one.

This chapter, in other words, is emphatically not about Cooking with Herbs or The Uses of Wine in the Kitchen— or any of the other parochializations of the great catholic truths of cookery. Cooking with Herbs is a silly subject. Of course one cooks with herbs—and with oil and vinegar, mushrooms and shallots, black bean and salted turnip—and calves' feet and fish heads besides. A cookbook should be about the ocean of cookery itself, not about the brooks that run into it. But more than that, it is a dangerous subject: it implies that there is such a thing as cooking without herbs —a proposition to which no thinking cook would give a minute's mindspace. And last, of course, it is a sad subject, as is Cooking with Wine, because one is forced—by the fact that there is actually a market for such books—to recognize that there are people who, having never cooked with either of those necessities, have therefore spent most of their lives not cooking at all.

You admonish me. I should not be so hard on innocent ignorance. But I am not. I am a teacher: an honest absence of knowledge in anyone draws me to him with enthusiasm and love. I always meet darkness with a candle, not a curse.

I am, however, relentlessly hard on teachers who are dim bulbs—who think that lighting one room takes care of the whole house. The Uses of Wine in the Kitchen, indeed! Wine has a use in every room in the house, not excluding the bathroom where, when the mouth wash runs out, you can always gargle with cognac. And in the kitchen, its first use is one such teachers almost invariably put last: the exhilaration of the cooks for their work.

But let them alone. Ours is the long subject of seasoning *tout court*. On with it.

In accordance with our principle of starting, whether up or over, from scratch, I want you now to strip your kitchen, mentally at least, to nothing. If you are in the first group, you begin that way in any case; if you are in one of the other two, you must, in this present exercise, join the first: it is they who are in the elegantly sacramental situation for our mutual refreshment.

With their tabula rasa before us, therefore, I suggest we make some lists. I shall comment as we go, but you must feel free to interrupt or disagree, to cheer, whistle, hiss, or boo as the mood strikes you. That way, it won't all be my persiflage.

First we must have water. All life is from the sea; if you collected all the water that goes up the chimney when a log burns, you could put the fire out in one shot; even you yourself, right along with the watermelon and the standing rib roast, are mostly H_2O. Desiccated, none of us would look like much. If your water bill is paid, however, we may take this fundamental seasoning for granted and pass on.

Next, salt, pepper, and sugar. Plain salt, if you please:

the iodized stuff has a nasty smell, particularly if you toast almonds in a panful of it. If you are worried about an iodine deficiency, eat fish, as God meant you to. If you live in the Arizona desert, buy tuna or canned mackerel. Anything is better than eating medicine. Pepper? Whole black pepper-corns only.

You object that you have no pepper mill. Ah! How easy it is for the mind to lose sight of its purpose. You not only have no pepper mill; at this moment, you have nothing but water and salt. I remind you, we are starting from scratch. As a good teacher, I am very patient, but I hope you will pay closer attention and try to avoid these lapses.

I require whole black peppercorns, freshly ground, because only they have the requisite fullness of flavor to qualify as seasoning. The preground sneezing powder in the super-market jars is only for playing mean practical jokes on other people's pillows.

How do you grind them without a grinder? You don't. You crush them. With what? With anything that works: a mortar and pestle, the flat of a knife, a hammer, a pot bottom, a rolling pin, a wine bottle, or a passing steam roller. The deep mystery of gravitational attraction—the love affair between the great mass of the earth and all other material things—is on your side: simply position your peppercorn be-tween two objects that want to get together more than the peppercorn wants to stay whole, and the job is done. Im-agination!

Sugar. For openers, just white, refined sugar. Oh, I know. Some of you are against that on nutritional grounds. You want brown sugar or honey. Well, take a substitute if you like, but I must remind you once again that you are close to getting away from the point. Here we are, barely into the introduction to the subject of seasoning, and off you go into a tirade about the outer reaches of nutrition. That will come, believe me. But cooking must come first. Sugar, at this basic level, is for sweetening. Unless you want every dish you sweeten to smack of the molasses factory or the bee-hive, stick to white sugar only.

The next group of seasonings to add to the list may strike you as odd or misplaced, but I ask you to bear with me. It is: onions, garlic, and lemons.

Notice how far we have come already. A can of evapo-rated milk and a palmful of rice will now give us a sweet rice pudding, redolent of the lemon rind we can chop fine and put into it. Working backward toward the beginning of the meal, three more palmfuls of rice, plus water, will give us a base for the main course. A little ground chuck, cadged from somewhere, shaped into patties, and rolled in crushed pepper, will yield hamburgers *au poivre*. Some minced onion, a bit of water, and a touch of lemon juice swirled in the pan make our gravy. Borrow some lettuce and we're home free: the bowl rubbed with a clove of garlic; the lettuce, washed, dried, and broken up; some thin-sliced onion thrown in for flavor; and the whole seasoned with salt and lemon juice and tossed.

You want oil in your salad? So do I, but we don't have any yet. Please do not get ahead of yourself. This is a leisurely exercise. Nothing in life should be allowed to pass untried just because something you're used to is missing. Salads with only salt and lemon juice are delightful—and nutritionally sound as well. Furthermore, if you cook your meat properly rare, there'll be enough grease in it to make up for any lack of oil. Admittedly, that's not polyunsaturated fat, but . . .

Ah, but you see? You have infected me with your habit of leaping ahead. Undisciplined minds, wandering imagina-tions! They snare us all. How hard it is for the cluttered to enter into the kingdom of simplicity!

We come now to three seasonings that, more than al-most any listed so far, are usually misclassified as ingredients: oil, vinegar, and wine.

For oil, I give you a choice: olive or peanut. Only one, though, if you will, for this is an exercise in simplification.

If I were forced to this extremity, I would choose olive oil, but by a very slight margin. You will do as you see fit, though I hope you will not be tempted to pick some tasteless *tertium quid* like corn oil. My point in including oil among the seasonings is that, even if it is used for nothing more than frying, it imparts flavor to a dish. How sad, then, when the bland is substituted for the distinctive. (I also hope that, if you choose olive oil, you will not succumb to the urge to save money and buy one of those salad mixtures that is 10 percent olive oil and 90 percent God knows what.) In any case, my reasoning in support of the choice of olive oil is as follows.

If I had to choose but one cuisine to the exclusion of all others, it would be the Chinese. Chinese cooking, however, requires an array of additional seasonings that is out of the question this early in our list. Accordingly, peanut oil, which is in many ways my first choice, goes by the board for now. With olive oil on hand, however, some of the best cookery in the world becomes instantly possible: the Spanish, the Italian, and above all, the Provençal. The price of olive oil, of course, puts deep frying in the shade for the moment—but then, there is no simplification without sacrifice. Pruning is, after all, pruning. On the other hand, if you can't live without your home-fried chicken and you don't mind the taste of peanut oil in your salads (I'm not wild about it, but it's certainly an acquirable taste) choose peanut oil and enjoy all the crispness you can get.

About vinegar, you must be equally jucidious. I live near an Oriental grocery, and therefore the cheapest, best vinegar in the world is always available to me: white Japanese rice wine vinegar. It's also carried by some supermarkets; get it if you can. On the other hand, if I had to do without it, I would, without hesitation, opt for plain old cider vinegar: It has a good, honest apple taste, and it goes with practically everything. I would stay a hundred miles away from distilled American white vinegar (tasteless) ; and five hun-

dred miles from anything labeled Wine-Flavored Vinegar: if
you read that label as slyly as the foxes who wrote it, you will
know instantly that it's nothing but plain white vinegar
souped up with red coloring and something that passes for
wine flavoring. Real grape wine vinegars are, of course,
available; but they are either expensive or, if cheap, poor.
Wine vinegar is never any better than the wine it's made
from; the wine the vintners sell to vinegar makers is usually
stuff they didn't have the gall to fob off on the drinking
public.

Which brings us, logically enough, to wine, and to a
list of possible alternatives at which the mind boggles. At this
point in our exercise, however, this is no *embarras de rich-
esses;* it is just another occasion on which our voluntary
poverty calls us to reduce the available many to the lonely
but omnicompetent one. What we want is a single wine that
will serve not only for all the purposes for which God gave
man the sauce but also, and principally, as a seasoning in the
kitchen.

You notice that I have avoided the circumlocution "fruit
of the vine." That is because the wine I choose for this list
is not made from grapes at all, but from rice: Japanese sake.
Once again, the margin of its advantage over other possible
choices is narrow in the extreme; but it's real, and I'm prepared to argue for it.

A wine to be used for the purposes of cookery (which
includes, naturally, the subject of drinkery as a necessary
adjunct of the *actus coquendi*) must have the following
properties:

1. It must be drinkable. There is no such thing in God's
mind as cooking wine. If there are any theologians present, I
shall refine that a bit and make a distinction: cooking wine
is known by God, but only by way of the permission he ex-
tends to those things that exist contrary to his primal will
(*sed tantum ad modum divini permissionis malorum*), it is

unknown by him *eo usque quod non convenit arbitrio divino* (because, in fact, it's no damn good) . It's salted. Anyone who could do that to good wine would salt his mother as well. Therefore, (*a*) no good wine is ever made into cooking wine by sane people and (*b*) no sane people ever drink the wine that the insane make into cooking wine. Sake is eminently drinkable. Hence the choice of sake.

2. It must be strong enough to keep well. Table wines (9 to 14 percent alcohol) do not stand up very long after opening. Even good claret, three days after the cork was pulled, is drinkable only as a matter of conscience. Accordingly, wines for cookery, because they will be around for a while, should have the alcoholic strength of the fortified wines (18 to 21 percent) . This narrows the field to port, sherry, Marsala, Madeira, vermouth, sake, Shaohsing, and the like. I choose sake because it has to some degree all the virtues of the rest and, at the same time, is not so replete with the distinctiveness of any of them that it loses its flexibility as an all-purpose seasoning. It has a touch of the sweetness of port and Marsala, a hint of the maderization of sherry and Madeira, the strength of a medium-dry vermouth (it also makes a good martini) , and the quiet authority of Chinese Shaohsing.

3. It must not be frightfully expensive. God loves a cheerful giver; the cook who has to be stingy with wine (a tablespoon in a stew) can hardly qualify for the divine pleasure. Furthermore, the bottle of sake in the cupboard stands as a perpetual guarantee that no guest, however unexpected, need ever be sent away totally parched. A good cellar may run out; but a good kitchen always has something in it.

III

THE REMINISCENT NOSE

good kitchen, however, needs more than the seasonings we've acquired so far. Our list to this point, like all foundations, is long on importance but a bit short on interest. Not that lemons, onions, garlic, vinegar, and wine can't produce some spectacular culinary results; it's just that they only whet the nose's appetite for the full range of smells—of fragrances, aromas, bouquets, redolences, pungencies, and reeks—that enter into good cookery.

Wine tasters use a vocabulary all their own when they do their work, and one word in particular strikes my fancy. When they speak of the smell of a wine, they subdivide it into *aroma,* the basic odor of the grape variety from which it was made, and *bouquet,* the distinctive and developed odor of the wine as wine. But for the single, overall, complex and combined fragrance that salutes the sense of smell like an army with banners, they speak of the *nose* of the wine.

So, too, in cookery. Every good dish has a *nose.* As does every good cupboard, pantry, kitchen, and house. And no seasonings contribute more to that grand and consolidated proboscis than spices and herbs. They—and the renewal of our attitudes toward them—need the better part of a chapter by themselves; taste would be a poor thing without them.

As a matter of fact, the true tastes—the sensations you can distinguish with your taste buds only, the flavors left to you when you have a bad head cold—are just four: salt, sour, bitter, and sweet. The rest of gastronomy addresses itself to the other senses: to touch, here for texture, as in the smoothness of a mousse, the granularity of bulgur wheat, the crispness of water chestnuts, and the hardness of pork crackling; to sight, as in the brown-gold of well-fried chicken, the brilliant contrast of green broccoli and yellow hollandaise, and the elegant arrangement of a platter of sliced Chinese pot roast with a border of quartered soft-center eggs and concentric circles of halved cherry tomatoes and scallions cut into flowers; to touch again, this time for temperature, as in the coldness of a good madrilene, the piping hotness of stuffed crêpes, and the astonishing combination of the two in hot Chinese apple fritters dipped in boiled sugar syrup and plunged into ice water; to hearing, for the voice of the fat that falls in the fire; and finally, of course, to the nose.

Interestingly, the true tastes can combine without interfering with one another: witness bittersweet chocolate, or sweet and sour pork. Indeed, in good cookery, they are almost always found in combination—the madrilene needs both the lemon and the salt; sweet desserts without any salinity at all are almost always a mistake. But the true smells are more temperamental. They need to be handled artistically, for they can easily cancel one another or produce the jarring effect of miscast sopranos. God loves a sweet-smelling savor; but he made a great many more smells than tastes, so there is more room in the nose than in the mouth for trespasses that incur the divine wrath.

Therefore, renewal is nowhere more necessary than in your approach to herbs and spices. Ours shall be a thoroughgoing and fundamental renewal—renewal by way of drastic pruning, or, to change the imagery, renewal by way of retreat.

I suggest that, no matter which of my three groups you belong to, you limit yourself at this point to only five herbs or spices. The number is arbitrary, and the choice of the particular five will be according to your own taste. We'll get to that in a moment. What is not arbitrary, however, is the retreat itself. We have all stocked our herb and spice shelves haphazardly: a jar of tarragon never used since we tried to duplicate Alice Frill's Tarragon Chicken (it wasn't really much of a recipe) ; some dill for Mackerel in Dill Sauce we had only that once; a box of whole nutmegs because Steve La Porta's grandmother always grated fresh nutmeg into her zucchini sauce for pasta, even though we never got around to it—all in all, several feet of shelving full of oddments that have piled up over the years and gone stale.

The crucial point is that those of us who have run kitchens for years (groups two and three) have never seriously developed either a philosophy or an art of using herbs and spices. Worse yet, those just starting out (group one), are more than likely to make all the same mistakes, beginning with the unthinking acceptance of the contents of the first gift spice rack. For all of us, therefore, the retreat to a bare five items is the only way.

And I mean retreat precisely in the religious sense of the word: a thoughtful withdrawal resulting in a radical renewal. This must be no merely mental diversion. If you have ever made a formal retreat, you are aware of how easily it can fall into just that: from Monday through Thursday, you think deep thoughts about the renovation of your life from the ground up; but on Friday morning, just before you have to leave at lunchtime, you give up on all that and settle for rearranging the same old furniture of your life. You make yet another revision of your chronically hopeless daily schedule, and never get past Saturday night with a single item on the list.

That is why I have chosen the number five as the maximum for spices and herbs on our list here. The rules for your renewal must be radical indeed if they are to have power enough to jolt you out of your worn but aimless ways. For your seasoning has become what it is precisely because you have been lawless—without rule—in the practice of it.

And lawlessness always produces two effects: first, it fosters chaos; but second, it induces in you a radical indisposition to rule as such. It is not that you have followed misguided precepts for herbing and spicing; were that the case, a mere apologia for a more excellent rule would probably suffice to bring you to repentance and a better mind. It is, rather, that you have no experience of rule at all in these matters—you wouldn't recognize a salutary injunction if it leapt up out of the pot at you. Hence, five only. Not five herbs and five spices; five all told. Given any more leeway than that, you will promptly relapse into your unthinking ways and never renew your grasp of seasoning at all.

I do not, however, want you to think that I am encouraging you to develop a legalistic attitude toward these things. We are not casting out the demon of herbal unrule so you can go and take to yourself seven devils worse. In the first place, this is only an exercise, not a way of life; and in the second, all rules, once properly forged and tempered, actually improve with a little flexing. Law is the shape of life; but it is not life itself. The man who bends the rules a bit almost always does so out of a consideration—at least as he sees it— of the pulsing, real beings underneath the formalities; the man who keeps them no matter what is always in danger of preferring shape to life—and of ending, accordingly, with nothing but creatures of air and darkness.

Again, therefore, five. Five only. And no cheating. That's final.

When you do cheat, however, cheat thinkingly.

The question now comes, which five—and on what basis is the selection to be made? As I said, the choice is yours to make, but let me point out the several principles by which you might come to a decision. As I see them, then, they are three: the intellectual, the practical, and the sensuous. Any one of them will do the trick; but if you want to work by a combination, feel free to do so.

The *via intellectus* first: Select the cuisine you would

least like to do without and stock your meager spice rack with the items most needed for that. I call this the intellectual way of going about it because the choice of a particular cuisine is largely a head trip. Good cooking of any school is always acceptable, and no eater worth his spice ever turns it down. The decision in favor of Italian or French, Spanish or Chinese cookery is made not on the basis of goodness of taste but on the intellectual appeal of the school's general theory and practice of cooking. Food is an exceedingly mental proposition; indeed, one of the marks of the born cook is the ability, even after a full meal, to launch enthusiastically into a discussion of other dishes, different recipes, and the menu for the next day.

As with all intellectual delights, however, one should not attach any eternal—or even too much temporal—weight to one's decisions about the cuisine of predilection. The mind, albeit one of the glories of man, has, since Adam's fall, been liable to error, ignorance, pride, and prejudice; it needs the discipline of constant openness. The wise cook will probably have at least half a dozen favorite schools of cookery in the course of a lifetime.

Nevertheless, if you currently have a strong candidate— if say, you have been on a binge of Italian cooking for a year now—it is perfectly proper to go with that *pro tem* for the purposes of your list. Or with any other that qualifies. Herewith, therefore, some personal, and not particularly authoritative, selections of five basic herbs and spices according to cuisine. Added to what we already have on the list, any one of them will satisfactorily put you in business. (A note: The runners-up given after each selection are the first items to buy, borrow, or filch when you cheat; the single recipe is intended to give you an idea of what can be done with the herbs and spices mentioned.)

1. *Italian* (general Southern/Northern mix) : basil, oregano, rosemary, bay leaf, and stick cinnamon.
Runners-up: thyme, nutmeg.

SPATCHCOCKED CHICKEN WITH RED SAUCE

☐ Brush a broiling chicken that has been split in two, or a whole chicken that has been flattened (see pp. 174–75), on all sides with olive oil, salt and pepper it, and roast it in a flat pan for an hour or so at 425°. Baste occasionally with a little white wine.

While the chicken is roasting, empty a large can of tomatoes into a saucepan and add the following: a pinch of oregano, 1 tsp. basil, and ½ tsp. rosemary, all pounded fine, the rind of half a lemon, a piece of stick cinnamon, a pinch of sugar (for directions on pinching, see p. 186), and some freshly ground pepper. Bring it all to a boil, chopping up the tomatoes in the process with a wooden spoon, and cook it down to something like two-thirds to half its original volume. Turn the fire off, stir in a generous lump of butter, and salt to taste.

During the last ten minutes of the roasting of the chicken, spoon the sauce around (not over) the chicken. Serve with buttered pasta.   ☐

2. *French* (also a general all-purpose selection) : thyme, marjoram, savory, bay leaf, and blade mace.
Runners-up: freeze-dried chives, tarragon, whole cloves.

A note is in order here. If you ever have the inclination and the space to grow your own herbs, do it. All fresh herbs have, above and beyond their principal aroma, additional fragrances so volatile that they are lost in the drying process, particularly if it is hurried along (as it is commercially) by heat. Fresh basil, for example, is astonishingly fragrant of anise. Even home-grown basil, just hung in the air till it dries naturally and then stored uncrushed in a tightly covered glass jar will, when you crush it in the palm of your hand over the salad, make the supermarket product smell like old tea in comparison.

WHITE STOCK

☐ Rinse well some raw chicken carcasses, or some raw pork or veal bones (for instructions on boning, see pp. 92–93), or a combination of all of them, and put them in a large pot with the following: some chopped carrot, onion, celery, and parsley, a crushed clove of garlic; a pinch of thyme, a bay leaf, a blade of mace, ½ tsp. each marjoram and savory, and a few whole peppercorns.

Add water to cover to the depth of your thumb, under-salt it, and simmer for 2 to 3 hours.

Strain; cool quickly, uncovered; and refrigerate promptly. Remove the fat when cold (if the bones were all chicken, you have chicken fat; if all pork, you have lard) and freeze the stock in containers (see pp. 176, 185).   ☐

3. *Spanish/Caribbean* (My own choice, in fact, when I was forced to the wall by the exigencies of a singles' apartment) : oregano, cumin, paprika, red pepper, and a jar of roasted sweet red peppers (change the water daily after opening; they'll keep a week or so).

Runners-up: saffron (when you end the austerity program, this will launch your poverty program), nutmeg.

If you choose this cuisine, your wine must be sherry. It is essential that this be borrowed as soon as possible: a small jam jar carried with you on all visits to friends will insure your supply until the austerities are over; accept, however, only honest, dry Spanish sherry—beggars are always choosers.

ARROZ CON GAMBAS

☐ Crush together ½ tsp. oregano, a pinch of cumin, a pinch of saffron (if you have it), and 1 tsp. salt. Add a splash of water to dissolve the salt, then a clove of garlic, a few sprigs of parsley (chopped), the juice of ¼ lemon and 1 T. olive oil, and mash all together.

Peel and devein a pound of raw shrimp, put them in a bowl, add the above, mix well, and let stand.

Coat the bottom of a Dutch oven or a deep frying pan with olive oil and add to it the following: 1 large onion (chopped), 2 T. minced smoked ham, 2 tomatoes (peeled and chopped), 1 sweet roasted pepper (chopped), 1 T. paprika. Simmer until the onion is soft.

Wash 1 cup long-grain white rice thoroughly, add it to the pan along with the shrimp, stir everything together to glaze, and add a cup or so of water. Salt to taste, bring to a boil, cover and cook over low heat for twenty minutes.

(With minor variations—like browning the chicken or the sausage—this recipe can be used with cut-up chicken, Spanish sausage, or squid. It would then give you Arroz con Pollo, con Chorizos, or con Calamares, as the case might be.)   □

4. *Greek/Armenian* (Middle Eastern, generally) : oregano, dill, cinnamon, mint leaves, and clove.
Runners-up: rosemary, nutmeg, thyme.

Another note: I have not required stick cinnamon and whole cloves in this list, but in the interest of flexibility, I urge you to purchase those, and not the ground forms. Buy your seeds whole too; eventually you'll force yourself into getting a mortar and pestle.

How do you grind whole cloves? The same way you crush whole peppercorns—with the flat of a knife under the palm of your hand. And stick cinnamon? Take a children's pocket pencil sharpener, wash out the graphite, make some cinnamon shavings, and then crush away as with the cloves. You are not lost. You are on the royal road to the Kingdom of Ingenuity.

IMAM BAYELDI

☐ Peel 3 medium-size eggplants and cut each lengthwise in 8 slices; soak in salted water for half an hour, and drain well.

Measure 1 cup olive oil and pour a little in the bottom of a casserole. Slice 3 or 4 large onions and the tomatoes from a large can. Arrange the eggplant pieces, the onions and the tomatoes in layers in the casserole, sprinkling each layer with the following: oregano, crushed garlic, chopped parsley, a pinch each of sugar and ground cinnamon, salt and freshly ground black pepper to taste, and most of the remaining oil, parceling everything out among the layers. Top with a layer of sliced tomatoes, and sprinkle with plain white bread crumbs and the last of the oil, salt, and pepper.

Bake, covered, for one hour at 350°; uncover and bake until tender and browned. Serve hot or cold.   ☐

5. *Swedish* (the taste of my childhood) : white peppercorns, bay leaf, whole cardamom seeds, dill weed, and a large, resealable can of whole Swedish anchovies sprats (not Italian anchovies—many different fishes are made into many different kinds of anchovies: the Swedish kind are in a sweet and spicy sauce; alternatively, you could buy a tube of Norwegian —not French, or any other kind—anchovy paste) .
Runners-up: almond extract, cinnamon.

ROYAL POT ROAST

☐ Brown all over in butter in a Dutch oven a piece of beef tied for pot-roasting. Add to the pot the following: a quart of milk, a generous tablespoon each of vinegar and medium Karo syrup, a bay leaf, a peeled onion, a dozen white peppercorns, 4 Swedish anchovies (you can remove heads, tails and insides if you like, but you don't have to), a shotglassful of cognac, if you have it, and salt to taste.

Simmer covered for three hours on top of the stove, turning the meat a few times. Strain and skim the gravy, thicken with flour and butter, and add heavy cream and salt to taste.   □

6. *Chinese* (The hardest of all the lists to reduce to five; but then, we already have garlic, and we can always buy scallions as a vegetable) : fresh ginger root, light soy sauce,* plain sesame oil, oyster sauce, dried black mushrooms.
Runners-up: dark soy,* red chili paste, dry mustard, hoisin sauce, brown bean sauce, salted black beans, salted turnip, wood ears, lily flowers, five spice powder—in general, the rest of Old Dead Ernest's fairly admirable list.

GAI FUN

□ Bone out the breast, second joint, and leg meat of half a broiling chicken. Dice the meat.

In a bowl, combine 1 T. peanut oil, 2 T. dark (or light) soy, two thin slices fresh ginger (minced), a small clove of garlic (minced), a few freshly crushed black peppercorns, a pinch of sugar, five large Chinese black mushrooms soaked in hot water for 15 minutes and diced, a piece of salted turnip (minced) —if you have it—and a generous splash of sake. Add the meat and mix well.

Wash 1 cup rice thoroughly, put it into a pot which will hold five times the volume of the rice, add water up to the first joint of your middle finger (see p. 13), cover, and bring to a boil. Uncover and let the surface water boil away.

Just before the water disappears down the holes in the rice, put the chicken and its marinade on top of the rice, re-

* Kikkoman Japanese soy sauce is the best substitute if you can't find the Chinese varieties.

cover the pot, and turn the fire down as low as possible. Cook
for 20 minutes, uncover, mix well, garnish with chopped
scallions, and serve. Pass the sesame oil—and the chili paste,
the mustard, the soy, the coriander leaves, the . . .   □

The second principle on which you might make your
selection of five is the practical, or, as it should more properly be called, the historico-pragmatic. It has the virtue of
totally circumventing the pitfalls of the intellectual approach: you can apply it in one minute, with your mind
closed down for the night. Admittedly, it will work only for
groups two and three, but even with that limitation, it may
well be the safest method of all.

Simply go to your present spice/herb shelf (either in
fact or in your mind) and make a note of which containers
are the emptiest and/or the most frequently in need of re-
supply. Number them in order of descending importance
and take the first five on the list. If you're moving, take only
those with you—holding onto the list, however, for informa-
tion as to runners-up. If you're in group three, trying for
renewal *in situ,* transfer the chosen five to a new location and
call that your spice rack for now.

By the way, don't store herbs and spices either in, on,
or over the stove. Remember the volatility of their fragrances. Find the coolest, driest place in the kitchen and keep
them there. Where? Well, obviously, not in the sunlight.
How about the dish closet? After all, it's only five items.

Again by the way, one of the side effects of the application of this second principle is the discovery of which cuisine
you do in fact practice—as contrasted with the several cuisines you think you practice when you're being intellectual
about your cooking. My own experience will illustrate. I
have already given you my abstract choice: the Chinese. And
indeed, since I have been more or less on my own, it is peanut
oil, sesame oil, black mushrooms, oyster sauce, soy, and
ginger root that I'm always running out of. But when I was

cooking for a larger household, the list was quite different. It was marjoram and savory (vast quantities of stock were always being produced), oregano and basil (if Long Island ever had an indigenous cuisine, it is now Italian, by a wide margin), and ground cinnamon (so much for the purities of the intellectual approach—I had cinnamon toast freaks in the house).

Make your own list, therefore, and meet the cook everybody else knows you to be.

The third principle by which you may select the fundamental five is the sensuous. Like the second, it is simplicity itself, but it makes more demands than either that or the first: it requires, in fact, that you put yourself in a meditative frame of mind.

Note first, however, that this exercise takes the form of a blind sniffing: you must tape over the name labels of all the items in your present collection of herbs and spices. Then, having seated yourself comfortably at the table, you set them out in front of you, together with a pad and pencil. Finally, writing a number on the first one you pick up and a corresponding number on the pad, you open the container and sniff the contents. If necessary, take a pinch or two and crush it between your fingers to release the full bouquet.

You must not, however, pick up the pencil too soon. The last thing I want you to do is write down what you think the name of the particular spice or herb is. I mean that literally: this is not a guessing game that you win by calling things correctly; it is an inner journey of self-discovery in which you must write only what you really think and know about the item in your hand. The only way you can lose is by faking your impressions. If you come up with nothing whatsoever about a particular herb, you are still a winner, having found out that for you, in your history to this point, it means nothing at all. The only reason for remembering its name would be to remind yourself that you have yet to make its acquaintance.

Therefore, sniff each one meditatively, and jot down on the pad your actual impressions of it. Any honest record of what comes to mind is 100 percent correct; there should be no editing for any reason. Most people, on smelling oregano, for example, will think, pizza. Do not try to improve on that by putting down something you think will have snob value, like, the white clam sauce at Luigi's. On the other hand, if that's what actually comes to mind first, by all means put it down.

And do not feel obliged to limit yourself to what you consider respectably culinary observations. The impressions you record should be as freely associative and as far-ranging as you can let them be. You are trying to find out not what this or that herb is in itself but what it is to you. If something reminds you of new-mown grass—or a paint factory on an off day, Nana's pantry, Uncle Joe's tobacco pouch, the first restaurant where you met your last love, or the last restaurant in which you saw your first—then that is what it is. Write it down. Properly pursued, this exercise should produce an avalanche of moods, an assortment of giggles, and perhaps even a tear or two. Because, of all the senses, the nose has the longest memory. You may not have smelled the reek of a city pier since you were five; but one whiff of it, even at the age of fifty, will take you right back, stunningly sometimes, to the precise emotional texture of that first moment.

So by all means take your time. An entire morning or a whole evening is not too much to give to this exploration of yourself. You have been eating for all your life. The depth and complexity of your nose's experience with these seasonings is matched by almost nothing else. Record, therefore, all the impressions you can, and only at the end write down what you think the name of each is.

When you have done them all, simply take the five items which are obviously the richest for you, and go with those as your spice shelf *in via*. If you find you don't know any recipes for one or two of them (that can happen: we are mysteries, above all to ourselves—it is possible to go on for years, not using what we really have or even missing what we really want), look some up. The goal of the exercise is enrichment, tailor-made to your taste. It is not self-improvement according to someone else's bright idea of what might be good for you, but the satisfaction of your longings in answer to the history that produced them.

By way of illustration, let me give you some jottings on the shelf full of herbs and spices I myself happen to have on hand at the moment. True to the principle of blind sniffing, I have recorded my impressions first and the names of the items last, except where the name itself was actually the first impression.

1. Swedish glögg; mixing plum puddings in Advent; my mother's pantry; beef stock simmering before a party, waiting for the shot of Madeira to turn it into Emperor Soup. *Clove.*

2. H. Roth & Son in Yorkville; chicken paprikash; goulash. *Paprika.*

3. Grass; onions; fresh straw; tea; sour cream. *Freeze-dried chives.*

4. Roast chicken basted with dry vermouth; Sunday dinner in a sunny dining room with small children and a good claret; making love afterward on the bedroom floor with my feet against the door to keep the children from bursting in; making tartar sauce; béarnaise sauce. *Tarragon.*

5. *Garlic powder;* other people's breath; homemade English muffin pizzas; homemade blue cheese dressing; a night of pizza, beer, and bishop stories in a Westhampton bar.

6. Making stock; tea; my own kitchen; the burnt-oil smell of certain parts of New York City on a cloudy day when someone is blowtorching paint off steel; marjoram—but marjoram doesn't have all those oily upper partials. *Thyme.*

7. Cookie dough; butter; toast; mixing plum puddings; Christmas. *Cinnamon.*

8. Greek salad; lamb; kzartma; avgolemono soup made with lamb broth. *Mint leaves.*

9. Saffransbröd; bouillabaisse; dinner parties; a forgotten bistro in the East Fifties; risotto Milanese; El Faro in the Village; Arroz con Gambas at home; the great adventure of young marrieds in the fifties by which we leapfrogged over our parents' cookery and reclaimed our grandparents'—in my case, of course, the Swedish; my aunt Edith. *Saffron.*

10. *Oregano;* salads; braised lamb shanks with onions and white wine; white clam sauce with whole garlic cloves; making ten pizzas in a row at home for an all-night poker game; the Italian pork butcher's *giardinera* salad; stuffed mushrooms.

11. Normandy sauce; zucchini sauce with cream; ricotta and mozzarella filling for cannelloni with green pasta. *Nutmeg.*

12. Spritz cookies at Christmas; my grandmother's kitchen; junket; marzipan; Mazarin cakes. *Almond extract.*

13. A sunny kitchen; making stock; hay; earth; wooden wine cases newly opened, back in the days when the bottles were packed in stitched straw jackets; marjoram—but marjoram is a bit more earthy and less spicy. *Savory.*

14. The smell of a Christmas tree in a closed room early in the morning; potato soup at lunchtime on a rainy day in Jackson Heights; curry; stock; five pounds of shrimp, cooked with a whole box of bay leaves; boiling lobsters; veal scaloppine with lemon sauce; pork livers wrapped in caul fat. *Bay leaf.*

15. Stale stuff—been around too long; a paint factory; New York City on a very rainy day; hay. *Sage* (make a note to replace).

16. Paint; the Caribbean; old San Juan on a gorgeous evening; chili powder; the sweaty smell of the boys' gym in P.S. 89, Queens; roast pork with moros y cristianos; New

York City in its Hispanic reincarnation; nokkelost. *Cumin.*

17. Sour cream; fish sauce; vinegar; lamb with dill; herring with dill; dillkaviar; homemade spanakopita; salads; chicken paprikash. *Dill.*

18. Christmas bread; judebröd cookies; lamb korma; rice pudding; a closed attic; Château Lynch Bages '61; Pauillacs in general; dinner at noon on Sundays after mass. *Cardamom.*

19. Hot apple charlotte with apricot rum glaze; Tarte Tatin; flan; my mother making cakes; cubes of sugar dipped in *Vanilla.*

20. Earth; stock-making; tea; marjoram; *Marjoram* at last.

21. Stale *Basil;* fresh basil in the summertime; pesto Genovese; tomato salads in August.

22. A roast beef dinner in Astoria in the summer of '54; it was ninety-five degrees in the apartment all night long, the gravy was one fourth rosemary and three fourths grease, I had four martinis before dinner, a bottle of hot Pommard with the meal, and cognac afterward—all of which I lost because the room kept insisting on revolving every time I tried to lie down on the bed; lamb; chicken; cinnamon, lemon, and thyme. *Rosemary.*

As you can see, the choice is as difficult as the exercise is revelatory. But to give it short shrift: tarragon, cumin, cardamom, bay leaf, dill, saffron, and oregano. What? That's seven? Oh, picky, picky. If we have to, take out the cardamom and the dill.

Suddenly, I don't like this game any more.

I was going to give you a list of additional seasonings that I consider essential to even the most modest kitchen, but your nit-picking legalism has put me off my form. My disquisition on butter and Smithfield ham will have to come later, if at all; right now, I need a restorative. Let me fetch the Calvados and give you a non-Chinese variation on the chicken and asparagus dish.

CHICKEN WITH ASPARAGUS REVISITED

☐ Poach for a few minutes some boned chicken breasts in good chicken stock to which a couple of bay leaves have been added. Remove the breasts from the pot before turning the fire off and, after they've cooled a bit, dice them, cover them, and set aside.

Likewise, set aside the pot of stock, uncovered.

Wash some asparagus spears, snap off the tough bottom sections, and cut them into short pieces. Melt half a stick of butter in a saucepan, add a little salt, and simmer the asparagus pieces in the butter over a low fire, covered, until just barely tender.

Take the asparagus pieces out of the pan, leaving the butter behind, and put them with the diced chicken.

Make an unbrowned roux of flour and the butter in the pan. (Rule: 2 T. each of flour and butter will thicken 1 cup liquid to the consistency of a sauce.)

Strain an appropriate quantity of the reserved stock into the pan, whisk smooth as it boils, cook for a bit, add the chicken, the asparagus and some heavy cream, and heat through. Season with salt, if needed, and freshly ground white pepper.

Serve over buttered toast or rice. ☐

(I hope you notice that boiling raw chicken breasts in stock clarifies the stock almost as well as egg whites do. That's because they're both full of albumen. If you ran that stock through a clean coffee filter and then chilled it, you'd have a lovely clear chicken aspic.)

Before you pick another bone with me, however, let me justify my writing of recipes without giving precise quantities for everything.

The purpose of this book is to establish or refresh your sense of yourself as a cook. I do not have in mind improving your ability to follow directions. That is strictly your department. Any idiot with half a measure of seriousness can follow directions; the mark of a wise man is his awareness that most directions are written by seriously idiotic people. He therefore ignores them when they become, as they always do, monomaniacally consistent.

How should I know how much salt you like in your cream sauce? Who am I to say how much gravy you should make for how much chicken? If it's come to my having to count out your toast points for you or tell you what quantities are sufficient for two, four, or six, then we are in bad shape indeed. When you cook for fifty, you measure because it saves time, avoids spoiling large quantities of food, and keeps the boss happy. But you're the boss here. Anything you spoil can be written off to experience and eaten as a penance, with no one the wiser but you. And if anybody's watching, you can always tell him it wasn't a mistake, just a change in plan.

Therefore, my recipes are written in such a way as to require you to be a cook, not a recipe-follower—to use your head, your hands, and all the senses God gave you, in order to produce food worthy of the name. Do that and you'll never fail. After all, when you study piano, playing a new passage badly is not a disaster; it's just the first step on the road to playing it well. So, too, when you play house: a few misfingerings on the range or at the cutting board are all in a day's occupation. As long as you don't end up with fingers missing, there's no harm done. Take it from the top again, *adagio,* and by and by you'll get it right *allegro.*

IV

THE GROANLESS BOARD

ll of which brings us, logically enough, to the next major subdivision of the subject of cookery: equipment. Somewhat less logically, but with an inevitability we learn early to expect in this vale of tears, we come to an area in which things have been egregiously mismanaged, not only as regards the actual items involved, but above all as touching the philosophy of cause and effect that should govern their employment. Once again, therefore, because there can be no renewal in practice without a prior refreshment of theory, I ask you to pay close attention while I make a short excursus.

When the Schoolmen, following Aristotle at a sometimes excessively respectful distance, spoke of *cause,* they spoke in Latin—which was a pardonable device, since the name of the game was High Middle Ages, and Latin was the lingua franca of the times. Unfortunately however, the phrase "lingua franca" led a good many of them to lapse into French at odd moments, and even into German or English. This produced a great deal of confusion and led, eventually, to the cancellation of the game altogether in favor of modern languages, Protestantism, The Age of Exploration, The Hundred Years' War, industrial democracy, nuclear physics, Marx, Freud, Adelle Davis, and Monty Python. The ultimate result (by a progress too convoluted to trace here) was to put the concept of *cause* in a deep shade and to give rise to Bertrand Russell, Max Planck, existentialism, the principle of indeterminacy, neo-orthodoxy, the double standard, and the sexual revolution.

Having thus used up the required topics on Part I of the examination, we may now turn our efforts toward getting Causality out of the shade and back into the sunshine for a nice tan before it's too late in the season and people just assume she'll never make it socially here on The Island.

It is not easy to say whether the Middle Ages ended because people got tired of making distinctions in Latin, or whether Latin ended because people thought the distinctions sounded better in French; but it doesn't really matter, because in any case the upshot was a definite decline in distinguishing. After all, when was the last time one of your dinner guests waved a finger at you and said triumphantly, *"Sed distinguo"*? Not recently, I should think.

Still, things often become unpopular for silly reasons. I mean, why don't people keep Pomeranians any more? Perfectly good dogs, a lot safer than bull mastiffs and not nearly as pushy as Siamese cats. And yet there it is: you've probably read a book by a Schoolman more recently than you've seen a Pomeranian, which is sad, because they pick up a fair amount of loose dust. Very good on parquet floors.

Nevertheless—or perhaps accordingly—*cause* (or *causa* as they called it) is defined as a *principium positivum unde aliquid procedit realiter secundum dependentiam in esse*. This really sounds best in Latin, so there's no point in spoiling things with a translation. Besides, in English it just sounds silly; in German, it sounds German, as does everything else (tyrannical language) ; and in French it manages to look Latin but sound lewd at the same time, which is a bit of a distraction if you're trying to get down to serious study.

More important for our purposes here is the fact that St. Otho Hufnagel—the famous Pomeranian Schoolman and founder of the order of eleemosynary mendicants called the *Sodalitas Hufnagliae,* or Confraternity of Indian Givers, because of their practice of immediately borrowing back anything they gave away—distinguished *Causa*'s several moods as follows. (The facsimile is of the original *Handschrift* in the Tübingen library.)

The only essential parts of this document are the items not crossed out by the Holy Doctor (Lucky Boy, as it happened, was no good on a wet track; arabic numerals didn't come along in time and the saint took a drubbing in the hog market; the unhappy and slurring personal references to the abbot and the prior were subsequently confessed; about the candles, we just don't know). As a matter of fact, not even all the uncrossed items are as important as he thought they were, since modern philosophers have tended to take a dim view of the *intrinsic* causes and to tap their feet annoyedly at all that *material/formal* wurst-slicing.

Which leaves us, fortunately, with only the distinction between *efficient* and *final* causes to fuss over.

What has all this to do with kitchen equipment, you ask? And not a moment too soon, for I am just about to get to it. Let me, following the holy footsteps of the Father Founder, give you what I have to say in schematic form. (I have, unlike him, erased the phone numbers and the grocery lists. Why lay the burden of total honesty on one's biographers?)

KITCHEN EQUIPMENT IN ITS CAUSAL RELATIONSHIP
TO THE WHOLE OF COOKERY

1. Final, final cause of cookery (*causa finalis ultima*) :
        the good pleasure of God
2. Not quite so final final cause of cookery (*causa finalis propior*) :
        the good pleasure of man insofar as he is the result of 1. above
3. Immediate final cause of cookery (*causa finalis proxima*):
        THE TABLE
4. Remote efficient cause of cookery (*causa efficiens exemplaris*) :
        the mind of the cook
5. Proximate efficient cause of cookery (*causa efficiens personalis*) :
        the cook
6. Immediate efficient cause of cookery (*causa efficiens instrumentalis*) :
        KITCHEN EQUIPMENT
7. Immediate final cause of immediate efficient cause of cookery (*causa finalis proxima causae efficientis instrumentalis*) :
        THE STOVE
8. Remaining causes of cookery (*causae reliquae*) :

REFRIG/FREEZER

KNIVES $\begin{cases} \text{Chinese} \\ \text{other} \end{cases}$

COOKWARE $\begin{cases} \text{Chinese} \\ \text{other} \end{cases}$

OTHER

9. Causes of noncookery (*causae confusionis*) :
    JUNK EQUIPMENT

At a glance, from nothing but the sheer Latinity and metaphysical succinctness of this analysis, you can see precisely what I am getting at. Just in case you don't, however, I have used capitals in the important places to catch your attention. In any event, it is the Table I want you to think about first.

I give the Table the primary place in this discussion of kitchen equipment because it is the nearest to hand of all the final causes of cookery, and because final causes—the purposes or ends which govern operations—must always be explicated with due regard to the ascending order in which they govern.

You bathe, for example. The *efficient* causes of your bathing are your hands, subserved by a number of instrumental causes: the tub, the water, the soap, the washrag, and the towel. But the *final* causes of your thus removing the day's grease and grime—the *reasons* for your soaking, the *goals* of your showering and singing—reign hierarchically over all the steps of the process, and they rise, by giant steps, to nothing less than the throne of God in every case.

Accordingly, let us ask why you bathe. And let us say in answer that you bathe for mere refreshment, to feel clean. But why do you want to feel clean? Because you are the kind of creature who delights in cleanliness. And why are you that kind of creature? Well, because your mother trained you to be so. But why did she train you thus? (You must not, at this point, slip into an infinite regress, explaining your mother by her mother, that lady by your great-grand-mother, and so on. That will explain nothing, it will simply put off indefinitely the discovery of any solid final cause for all the other causes and land you in a dismal mental universe where there is a cause for everything except Everything, and therefore no real reason for anything.) The only ultimate explanation is that you and she are both creatures of a Creator who runs the world by delight, and that your delight in the bath has, as its final cause, nothing less than the good pleasure of God.

Change the answer a bit. Say that you bathe because you have a date. But why be clean for a date? Because you want to be pleasing to your companion. But why do you thus cherish companionship? Well, to shorten the story, be-cause the Word and the Spirit, the Second and Third Per-sons of the Trinity who bring you into being out of nothing, do so because of their companionable delight in the Father's pleasure—which delight you share because you are made in the societal image of all that divine sociability.

So, too, with the Table. It is the immediate reason for cooking. It stands in your home as the nearest of all those final causes that stretch outward and upward above it. The Table is for dining; dining is for your pleasure in company; companionship makes you friends in love; and love makes you friends with God. It is the first and simplest sacrament of all the rest, and therefore it deserves the place of honor: a careful consideration before even a word is said about a single efficient cause of cookery.

Notice how easily its omission would lead us astray. Let us answer the question, Why cook? with a less perfectly sac-ramental final cause. Let's say, for example, We cook in order to eat. But why eat? To stay alive. But why stay alive? In order to, etc., etc., right on up to, Because God made us that way. But do you see what we have done? We have left our-selves with a chain of causalities which make us no different from pigs. We have missed altogether our distinctiveness as human beings. Reaching God is easy; all final causes do that. But if you get the closest one wrong, you can very easily miss the uniqueness God has in mind for you.

Man is the animal who cooks his food. Yes. But man cooks his food because he is the only animal who *dines*. Eating peanuts out of a bag on the kitchen counter is not a human act; but eating Chicken with Peanuts, Kung Po Gai . . .

CHICKEN WITH PEANUTS (KUNG PO GAI)

□ Marinate (see p. 11) some boned chicken (2 breasts or the equivalent) cut into ½-inch dice.

Mince several cloves garlic and a generous slice of fresh ginger. Soak 8 dried Chinese black mushrooms in hot water for 15 minutes and dice; cut 2 scallions into matching short pieces. Have at hand peanut oil, ½ cup hot stock, the sake bottle, the jars or cans of brown bean sauce and hoisin sauce, the bottle of hot sesame oil, a solution of cornstarch and cold water for thickening, and a handful of blanched peanuts.

Heat the wok very hot, add the garlic and ginger and stir-fry for 10 seconds. Add the chicken and a splash of sake and stir-fry for 30 seconds. Add the stock, mushrooms, scallions, brown bean sauce, hoisin sauce, and hot sesame oil, all to taste. Boil, add the peanuts, thicken judiciously with the cornstarch solution, check the seasoning, and serve.   □

But of course, you see my point: a bit of that, on a proper table, in a nice dish, with a bowl of rice, a glass of beer and a long chat where love is . . . Why, you don't even need to think about final causes; you're practically home already.

You must also understand, however, that when I list the Table as the immediate final cause of cookery, I mean *the* Table—the board, groaning or otherwise, on which you yourself regularly dine. It does not matter whether that table is in the kitchen or the dining room; the only thing that matters supremely is that it *be*—and that you deliver to it everything you cook. If your home has several tables, the delivery should, of course, always be to the best and most considerable of them. Why prefer a lesser sacrament to a greater?

Unfortunately, though, the question is not as rhetorical as it sounds. For all the money we lay out on living arrangements, we often live foolishly. People too commonly use their dining rooms and living rooms only for company, thus giving themselves the demeaning impression that they do not, save with relative strangers, either dine or live in their own homes. But that is sad, and it is a direct cause of wretched cookery and bad manners. Deliver what you cook then, to the best place you can manage, and both you and it will be the better for the effort.

A word, however, is in order about the possible temptations to dereliction in the use of the Table which our several groups may experience. Those just starting out, for example, probably have the easiest time of it: with no bad habits of their own to plague them, they need be on guard only against that self-conscious smallness of mind which will whisper, "Pretentiousness!" in their ear. Their answer to such insinuation must always be, "Dry up! We are pretenders to a throne here." And their way of escape from temptation must be a deliberate aggravation of their offenses against such mean-spiritedness: cloth napkins, not paper; the good flatware; and always, without exception, a tablecloth. Place mat maketh not a place. There is napery at the Supper of the Lamb: the fine linen is the righteousness of the saints.

It is groups two and three who must expect the major temptations: Ernest's lady, for example, with her reluctance to fuss after a day of recalcitrant third-graders; or the new widower with his apprehensions about sitting alone where so lately, he feels, he sat in company better than his own. But that is all false. Rising from the dead is always a bother; and if we were good enough company for others, we can certainly, with a little effort, be good enough for ourselves. Otherwise, we defile their memory by insulting their taste in friends.

Let me pause for a moment and speak a word only to group two—to those starting over after some kind of death. In fact, let me speak only to the newly divorced, in order to make my point as clear as possible.

The world, oddly enough, does not take kindly to resurrections. The authorities not only sought to kill Jesus; they also tried their best to do in Lazarus as well. I thought about that for years, but never came up with any better understanding of it than the idea that it had something to do with destroying the evidence of Jesus' power. It was only after I myself had died the strange death of the divorced—and been raised by an even stranger resurrection—that I finally saw what must have been the real reason: the risen dead are tolerated only as long as they are careful not to look too obviously raised. The trouble with Lazarus had to have been that he refused to be discreet about being alive. Had he gone to just one or two small dinner parties and done a respectable revived-corpse act, they might have put up with him. But no. Instead, he dined regularly six nights a week, ate like Diamond Jim Brady, drank Calvados till two in the morning, and laughed all night at his own dialect jokes.

You will be asked, sometimes politely but always firmly, not to look too alive: Lazarus at dinner confuses the troops. And yet, what is there to do? Act as if you were still in the grave? Carry a little flacon of *eau de tombeau* in your purse? Of course not. You have been given a new life; flaunt it. And flaunt it above all to yourself. Sadness and guilt are facts; but forgiveness—especially forgiveness of yourself—must always be the largest fact. Embarrassment at the richness of your own existence is a loser. It should be rebuked the minute it rears its silly head. Napery, therefore, and stemware; and no skulking around eating self-pity out of pots. But always, always the Table.

Just a word to group three, and we're ready to move on. Someone wise once said that in the order of nature, place creates persons, but in the order of grace, persons create place. We have our being because the localities and temporalities of the world have allowed us houseroom for a while; but we live and find ourselves only because we have made for ourselves places by grace and love. Heaven is Someplace, not because it is localizable in terms of space but because it is full of persons, each of whom finally is Somebody worth taking a walk with through the Wood of Life on the way to the Wedding Feast, where a place has been prepared for us by the Lamb and his Bride.

You who are content in the places you have made—whose children, perhaps, are like olive branches round about your table, whose wives wear silk and purple, and whose husbands' love has no bitterness—you who have created these homes on the road to the House of Many Mansions—first of all, rejoice. You have a half nelson on the many-splendored thing.

But second, get your theology straight: creation is not a one-shot deal. God didn't make the world once upon a time; he makes it now, and new, at every moment. If he wanted to destroy it, he would not, according to the Angelic Doctor, have to do anything; he would have to stop doing something.

So with you. You did not set up your house once upon a time, years ago. You set it up every morning, new as the love your uprising proves. And precisely because it is such a long and constant work—and because there are so many hard things you need to do to keep the wolf of chaos from the door of your cosmos—you must be careful not to omit that which is easiest: a due regard for your daily downsitting around the Table.

I do not know in detail where you are; but I do know where America is, and it's not at home. Takeout food ingested from bags; TV dinners in front of the Monster; diet soda and single-wrapped cheese slices eaten on one foot at the kitchen counter. Ask yourself how many of these declinations from the act of creation you allow in your vicegerency. Is the sit-down family dinner a thing on your daily agenda, or a thing of the past? The Colonel creates only for the Colonel; Jack-in-the-Box is Pandora's box if you open it either mindlessly or often.

You need a day off, you say—after all, God has his Sabbath. But watch your theology again. God doesn't put creation on hold one day a week; he rests. He doesn't let up; he *recreates*. And while you are not required to put in hours like that, you would do well, in your role as lord of the domestic creation, to remember that convenience food is inconvenient to the work of your hands. Burger King has no throne for you to pretend to.

I knew all that once, and a great deal more besides. And I also forgot all that once—to the disgruntlement of all concerned. But under the Mercy, it looks as if I shall have another go at it, so all is not lost. A somewhat more expensive go, no doubt. But then, as Ernest says, It's not for poor people. Grace isn't cheap; only good.

If you're still on your first, bargain dose of it, therefore, cut those losses, group three, and get back in the creating business where you belong.

V

ASSAULT ON THE BATTERY

Isaid I knew all that, and a great deal more besides. Since we are on the subject of equipment, let me, by way of establishing my credentials as a working cook, give you a quick rundown of the items of hardware, woodware, and otherware with which I worked for more than twenty years. While they are not among the things I've forgotten, they definitely come under the heading of things I left behind. Still, the list should not be depressing, but encouraging—to group one because I am in fact doing without so much of it for now, and to groups two and three, because the necessity of doing without it has been the mother not only of invention but of a refreshed appreciation.

First, therefore, a glimpse of what I had; second, a list of what I've got; and finally, as always, the philosophy of it all.

And that's just from sitting here trying to remember it all. I'm sure I've left out plenty—including all the gadgets that just hung on the wall and stared reproachfully because they weren't used.

Oh. There were also two sets of stainless steel flatware, three sets of dishes (the main one with service for twenty-four), and enough stemware to serve six wines for upward of twelve people. (Everything started out at twenty-four pieces, but the breakage was as uneven as it was prodigious —claret glasses, I think, were the ones in shortest supply. On the other hand, N.Y. Mets gas station glasses—ten-ounce, roly-poly, ugly-smoky—seemed to go on forever. So did the twelve-ounce sour cream jobbies with daisies.)

OLD KITCHEN

Category	Items	Comments
Stove	*Garland* (gas) 6 burners 2 ovens (24″ × 24″) Broiler (20″ × 20″) Griddle (24″ × 24″) Ronson Table Chef Hibachis (3) Charcoal grill	It was black—and it got blacker over the years. But that was the best part; as long as the dirt wasn't a fire hazard, you just ignored it. Oven cleaning is a make-work operation invented by the devil.
Refrigeration	2 GE Refrig/Freezers 1 GE Upright Freezer	These were enough only at times. For large parties, we filled the bathtub with ice. For medium-size bashes, we put the beer in the clothes washer and laid the ice on top. (This was dangerous: There was usually at least one clown who couldn't resist putting the machine on spin.)
Plumbing	Pot Sink Bar Sink Automatic Dishwasher	I always wanted a water tap over the stove, but somehow never got around to it.
Knives, etc.	Chinese cleavers (5) French chef's knives (4) Butcher's knives (8) Paring knives (5) Roast beef/ham slicers (4) Bread knife Swivel parers (3) 24″ cabbage slicer Cucumber slicer Beef & potato slicer Carving sets (2) Poultry shears	These tended to be large: e.g., 14″ French knife, 12″ butcher's scimitar, 12″ straight butcher's knife, and fairly heavy cleavers.

Category	Items	Comments
	Scissors (3) Vegetable cutters Butcher's saws (2) Graters (6) Food mills (3) Spaetzle mill Spatulas (3) Steel spoons & forks (3 ea.) Gas station steak knives (24) Pastry scraper Sharpening stones (2) Butcher's steels (3)	
Cookware	Heavy duty aluminum pots (14)	These went from 30 qts down to 1½ qts by steps, with duplications toward the bottom of the list. There was nothing lined with teflon.
	Flat pans, etc.:	The largest, alas, usable only in a commercial oven. *Sic transit gloria.*
	Baking pans, from 23″ × 18″ × 4″ down (10) Paella, 14″ (2) Bread pans (6)	Among these were two antique covered round loaf pans that produced crusty loaves that looked like giant cough drops.

	Cookie sheets (4)
	Flan rings (4)
	Molds, various (7)
	Stainless steel:
	  Sauce pans (8)
	  Kettle
	  Double Boiler
	Cast Iron:
	  Frying pans (7)
	  Dutch ovens (2)
	  Omelet pans (2)
	Scandinavian:
	  plättar pan
	  egg pan
	  waffle iron
	  krumm irons
	  krustader irons	

Category	Items	Comments

	Woks (plus tools)
	    21"
	    14"
	    10"
	Double Chinese steamers:
	    16"
	    12"
	Copper:
	    Oval sauté (2)
	    Oval au gratin, 20"
	    Zabaglione pot
	Ceramic:
	    Porcelain casseroles (8)
	    Large au gratin (5)
	    Individual au gratin
	        6" (24)
	        5" (24)
	    Individual covered
	        marmite (12)
	    Custard cups (24)
	    Quiche/tart/pie (5)
	    Coffee pots (3)
	    Tea pots (4)	

Mechanical	Commercial slicing
	    machine
	Commercial meat grinder
	Mixer (hand)
	Blender
	French fry cutter
	Toasters (2)
	Coffee makers (2)
	Noodle machine
	Apple corer/parer/
	    slicer
		The electric knife—an abomination—was never used. The electric can opener gave out early on as a can opener, but continued in its retirement to function as what it really is after all: a cat-calling machine.

Other	Sieves (6) Collanders (2) Mixing bowls (8) Whisks (4) Ladles (7) Turners (2) Mortars (5) Skewers (innumerable) Larding needles Wooden spoons (2 doz.±) Salamander	Including a gorgeous big *chinois*.

Category	Items	Comments
	Noodle pins (2) Pastry pins (3) Pastry bags (6) Pastry tubes (lots) Cream roll forms (24) Cream horn forms (24) Cannolli forms (12) Pastry cutters Cutting boards (6—from 48″ × 30″ on down, including a Chinese log) Corkscrews (4) Pepper mills (5)	The best of the lot was a big cast iron job. I've never seen it on the market again. Had I known, I'd have bought a half-dozen.

PRESENT KITCHEN

Category	Items	Comments
Stove	Welbuilt (gas) 4 burners oven, broiler	I lucked out on this one, the whole apartment being heated by gas. The winter fuel bill was horrendous, but at least my record is still intact: I have never been forced to live with an electric stove, *Deo gratia*.
Refrigeration	GE Refrig/Freezer	
Plumbing	One regulation sink; no etc.	
Knives, etc.	Chinese cleavers (3)	The cleavers (except the largest) were bought new. I refuse even to attempt to live without them: austerity is one thing, but camping out is too much. For paring, I use my Swiss army knife.
	Bread knife Gas station steak knives (6)	

Category	Items	Comments
	Oddments (6 found, from sub-leaser—all wretched) Sharpening stone Butcher's steels (2) Corkscrews (2)	There's one on the Swiss army knife, of course, but I also pocketed the best of the lot on the way out.
Cookware	Wok & tools (14″) 12 qt. stockpot Iron frying pans (2) Iron Dutch oven (1) 1 set department store cast aluminum (6 pcs. came from landlord—not bad) Coffee pots (3, filched) Tea pot Odd pots (4, found—all exasperating)	
Mechanical	None	
Other	Cutting boards (2)	One of these is Chinese, i.e., a 7″ thick slice of maple log. Actually it's sycamore, which was what my oldest son had on hand when he got his chain saw and made it for me.
	Wooden spoons (5) Steel fork, spoon, and turner Whisk Sieve, collander Mortar Pepper mill	

I suppose the first thing to say about kitchen equipment is a concession. In a pinch, you can cook on anything, in anything, and with anything, provided it doesn't explode, leak, catch fire, or dissolve.

Having said that, however, I hope we can agree that it

will be the last instance of smallness of mind we will allow in our discussion. We are not trying to make do here; we are trying to do well on the smallest possible basis. Indeed, many of us should be aiming even higher: to do better than we ever did before, precisely because the removal of clutter has forced us back to the roots of our cooking. We are called to a new and deliberate beginning in which theory will not be buried under a heap of practice, nor practice be led six ways for Sunday by a multiplicity of theories.

Accordingly, let me take up in order the major headings I've used so far and comment on them in a format I think will be useful. I shall address myself first to the purpose, or final cause, of the equipment under consideration; second, to the selection of the optimal piece or pieces for our particular and limited purposes here; and third, to some warnings about the traps, pitfalls, lions, and dead dogs that lie so thick in the way of genuine renewal.

This last, by the way, is especially important. Unless you have been a careful student of man's stewardship of creation since Adam's fall, you may be tempted to think that such simple questions as What is the best stove to cook on?, What is the best pot to do it in?, and What is the cleverest knife to get it ready with? would have been answered once and for all not many days after the saber-toothed tiger got discouraged by the fire in the cave doorway and left man free to wrestle more with his identity than with his safety. But that just isn't so. The questions have indeed been answered—very often to perfection—but mankind has had a hard time keeping the answers in mind. History, in its sadder manifestations, consists largely of forgetting the lessons there was every reason to remember. T. S. Eliot, once more:

> . . . *what there is to conquer*
> *By strength and submission, has already been discovered*
> *Once or twice, or several times, by men whom one*
> *cannot hope*

To emulate—but there is no competition—
There is only the fight to recover what has been lost
And found and lost again and again: and now, under
    conditions
That seem unpropitious. But perhaps neither gain nor
    loss.
For us, there is only the trying. The rest is not our
    business.

Unfortunately, however, it is very often in the interest of somebody else's business to make a buck by selling you kitchen equipment that is either the wrong answer or no answer at all to the need it purports to fill. Hence the necessity of putting you on guard: in some categories, well over half the items available are no more suited to their purpose than a pair of cement swimfins.

And nowhere, perhaps, is this more true than on the subject of stoves. Man has cooked for as long as he has been man; stove manufacturers have not turned out workable stoves with anything approaching that consistency. Why, do you ask? Well, Original Sin, I guess. Nothing else can possibly account for the monumental missing of the obvious on display at every appliance dealership in the land. Only the tragedy of the Fall can explain this penchant for answering the wrong question first, and the right question—if at all—wrong.

You are not convinced? To persuade you, let me take you through the subject of stoves by two routes. The first is simple, direct and short—a triumph of the obvious culinary consequences of the discovery of fire. I give it to you in schematic form:

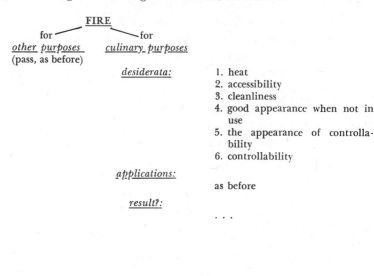

FIRE

for ——————for
other purposes   *culinary purposes*
(pass)

desiderata:
1. heat
2. accessibility
3. controllability

applications:
4. heating things in utensils
5. heating things in open flames
6. heating things in closed chambers

result:
a stove, which, in response to 1, will be fired by something that gets hot; to 2, will be in the house, not the yard; to 3, can be turned off and on at will; to 4, can put fire *under* things in pots; to 5, can direct fire *at* things in the nude; and to 6, can heat air hot enough to roast things whole

Quite plainly, a simple following through of this prospectus will produce, after enough miles on the road of human progress, the gas range—to which the wood stove, the coal stove and the oil stove historically gave place, largely because human beings, being lovers of flexibility, found it more sensitively controllable than anything else.

Look next, however, at a second bill of particulars—one containing some wrong, and loaded, desiderata:

FIRE

for ——————for
other purposes   *culinary purposes*
(pass, as before)

desiderata:
1. heat
2. accessibility
3. cleanliness
4. good appearance when not in use
5. the appearance of controllability
6. controllability

applications:
as before

result?:
. . .

Follow that one through and you get the electric stove or, worse yet, the electric ceramic cooking surface, neither of which, from a cook's point of view, is a serious improvement over the coal stove. You can't turn the things on fast enough to satisfy the need for an accessible fire; and once they're turned on, you can't shut them down fast enough to have a controllable one. You do, admittedly, have plenty of attention to *desiderata* 3, 4, and 5: little removable drip pans, your choice of decorator colors, and instrumentation that looks like the result of a marriage between a juke box and the dashboard of a DC-10. You also have an oven and a broiler that work. But that's about it. You emphatically do not have a whole stove that is responsive to the sum of your needs as a contemporary cook. You are back with your great-grandmother or your cave-uncle, tapping your foot impatiently while the fire heats up, and then hauling pots off the coals when they boil over.

You say that isn't quite true? You claim that one can learn to time his operations to the pace of an electric stove and so avoid exasperation? No. Quite wrong. *You* can learn, if you like; I will not, voluntarily at least, make a single effort in that direction—any more than I would spend even a minute trying to play the flute with mittens on. And I suggest that you develop the same attitude. The necessities of momentarily straitened circumstances may force you to make peace with oppression for a while—grace in the presence of adversity is always worth cultivating. But I am not concerned here with the further reaches of your spiritual life; I want you to be a *cook*. I urge you, therefore, to aim only at cooking with gas. Just be persistent. Sooner or later, you'll get there.

What do you do in the meantime? Well, first, I would suggest you try conning the landlord into installing—or at least allowing you to install—a gas stove. It can be done; in fact, I have just done it with my future landlord. A good cook needs more brass than just the rivets in his bread knife.

But if that is impossible, you must compose yourself and make do with your electric stove. I have a few suggestions. For one thing, I take back what I said just now about timing one's operations to the agonizing unresponsiveness of electric burners. I have done it for weeks at a time on summer vacations, and while it is a royal pain, it is no more so than much of the rest of life. Crosses must not be sought: that is mere masochism, if not spiritual presumption. But unavoidable ones should always be offered up with grace and good humor.

Second, however, you would be wise, if you have been reduced to cooking with electricity after long experience with gas, to alter completely your mental attitude toward the thing that has been foisted on you in the name of a stove. It will simply be an endless nag to continue thinking you have a stove to cook on; for alas, you know what a stove is. Accordingly, you must think of the device in your kitchen as a very clean, fairly safe, multi-burner hibachi.

Notice what that does. You no longer fret about the laggard way it heats up: a hibachi takes even longer—unless you're one of those people who habitually serve steaks au charcoal lighter. And you are freed from vexation when you have to take pots off the fire to control the heating: of course you must—that is the nature of a hibachi. With the proper attitude, you see, you can conquer the beast. You will even be able to do what less flexible cooks claim to be impossible: cook Chinese dishes in a wok. You simply turn the largest burner up as high as it will go and then make believe you are on the beach, holding the wok with a potholder and putting it on and off the fire as necessary.

Flexibility has its upper limits, however, and I am afraid I have not a single kind word to say about the ceramic cooking surface. It is simply some noncooking engineer's bright idea of a stove. It is not a cook's idea of anything. As a matter of fact, it strikes me as nothing more than a picture of a stove, with its little drawings of burners, frequently not quite ac-

curately located over the heating elements they hide. And if
the electric stove is slow, how much slower, to the point of
intractability, must this be; it is nothing more than an electric stove with a piece of crockery interposed between the
burners and the pots. You want to bring something to a boil
and then reduce it to a simmer? What you must do is switch
on two burners at once, the front one turned high for the
opening exercise and the back one turned low for the con-
tinuation. But that isn't cooking anymore; it's outsmarting a
gadget designed to solve a few unimportant problems at the
price of abolishing the necessary functions of the device.

How can such a thing happen, you ask? How can grown
men, trained in engineering and design, seriously offer the
public a product whose form continually contradicts its function? If you have to ask, you have failed to observe that the
trouble lies in the grown men themselves. The phrase is almost a contradiction in terms. "Grown women" is an accurate description, in most cases at least, for women, by and
large, do actually grow up. They play dolls for a while, but
then, with the competence that comes with adulthood, they
put away childish things, have babies, and stop the irrespon-
sible horsing around. If they designed stoves, I'm sure they
would simply design stoves and just get on with the cooking.

But grown men are always, at some not very deep recess
of their nature, just overgrown boys. They never lose the
sometimes charming but incipiently monomaniacal tendency
to take one lonely thought and extrapolate it to cosmic proportions. It's harmless enough when they're little, or poor, or
both: all it produces then are sand castles, baseball card col-
lections, and excessively complicated round games. But when
they become big and get adequate financing . . .

Three illustrations should suffice.

First, the Pringle, or imitation potato chip: I am sure
it is a perfectly normal thing for any boy, undergrown or
overgrown, to have invented. It answers, after all, every
boyish need. To begin with, it is an imitation: since boys are

never content with any act of creation except their own, it provides them with the reassurance that in spite of what Mother thinks, they actually have gone God and Daddy one better. Next, it is a tricky imitation, involving gratuitous difficulties—like whistling bird calls with a mouthful of saltines: the potato is not simply chipped and fried; it is chipped, dried, powdered, mulched, re-formed into a chip—*then* fried. But last, it has the all-important, mind-tickling difference from the real thing: Pringles are shaped like tiny saddles and nest perfectly. They no longer taste like potato chips, of course—unless you think, as boys do, that the essence of potato-chip taste is grease and salt. But that is a price they gladly pay for the triumph by which ingenuity has created something no one ever thought of even wanting.

It's not all bad of course. If they ever do grow up, their cleverness produces things like *Macbeth,* the steam engine, the Sistine Chapel, and the double-belled euphonium. The danger to sanity comes when overgrown boy inventors make common cause with overgrown boy financial wizards and are put in a position to perpetrate indefinitely what should have been nothing more than a summer afternoon's diversion.

The second illustration is the ceramic-topped range. Look, Mom! Two perfectly machined surfaces! No hot spots! Absolutely uniform heat transfer! And no spaces for things to fall into! Easy cleaning! Attractive appearance! To all of which Mom, with a yawn of sanity, responds, "Uh huh. Did you peel the potatoes?"

The third illustration is the greatest Boy Scout adventure of all time, the United States' involvement in Southeast Asia. You can work that one out for yourself. The big difference is that Mom didn't yawn. She cried.

I told you cooking was sacramental, a real presence, on the road, of the home the road goes to. Just add to that a constant reminder that the road, like the stick, has two ends —and that only one of them is labeled Heaven.

We need a happier subject. I was going to do cutlery

next, but let's set that aside for a moment and talk pots. At
least they're a bit less grisly than knives. And furthermore,
here is a subject in which practice has not wandered as far
from theory as it has with stoves. A few rules and applications
should do the trick.

Rule 1. A pot must be larger than you think. By way of
redressing the imbalance created by my critical remarks
about the male sex, it must be said here that women are the
chief offenders against this precept. If you want me to be
strictly accurate, I shall say "the female cooks of my acquaintance," but I still think I have a point. Admittedly, women
tend to think small in this department for perfectly natural
reasons: the smaller pot is easier to handle on the stove, and
it is less of a bother to clean up afterward in a crowded sink.
But notice, please, the rather male note of *idée fixe*—the
penchant for exalting the irrelevant accident over the ger-
mane substance—that underlies such an attitude. A pot is to
cook in; handling and cleaning must be kept firmly in second
place. Yet if you give a woman a pair of chicken carcasses and
turn her loose to make stock with a choice between a three-
quart and a twelve-quart pot, she will almost always use the
smaller—which, after the addition of onions, carrots, celery,
and parsley, has precious little room for the all-important
water.

Application 1. Therefore, if you're going to have only
five pots (a ridiculous limitation, I admit, but how else renewal?), the actual pot-type pots may be no more than two—
a twelve-quart (or larger) stockpot and a 1½- or 2½-quart
saucepan. You must, you see, conspire against your less worthy
tendencies as a cook. You must leave yourself no open avenues but the best.

Rule 2. Pots must be as heavy as possible: restaurant-
gauge aluminum, thick enamelware, ceramic-coated cast iron,
cast aluminum, cast iron, copper-clad stainless steel. Obedi-
ence to this commandment gives you two advantages. First, it

provides you with pots that will last indefinitely, unless you back the car over them; second, it solves the problem of uneven heat transfer, which little Johnny thought you had to destroy the stove to conquer. Your spaghetti will not stick, your rice will not burn, and your sauces will not have arcane black designs at the bottom.

Application 2, accordingly, enlarges the number of our utensils to four. We add a nine- or ten-inch cast-iron frying pan, and a three-quart cast-iron Dutch oven with a glass cover. Once properly seasoned, of course, these will never be washed with soap, only rinsed and scrubbed with cold water and a plastic scouring ball. And they will never be put away without first getting a few drops of healing cooking oil gently massaged over their inner surfaces. With that minimal care, however, they will almost certainly be part of your estate when your grandchildren set up housekeeping; and in the meantime, you get to eat all the pot roasts, stews, casseroles, paellas, cassoulets, eggs Benedict, and grilled cheese sandwiches you want.

Rule 3. There must be one truly versatile pot to serve all other purposes. It is unnecessary to discuss this theoretically at all. We may proceed directly to

Application 3. You must have a wok.

I do not propose here to tell you how to stir-fry things in the Chinese manner. A little later, perhaps; but I've already given you an idea of it, and anyway, many woks now come with an instruction booklet, which, whatever its shortcomings, will be enough to get you going. Let me instead tell you what to look for when you buy one, and then simply hymn its versatility.

All previous rules apply: i.e., your wok must be as large as is conveniently possible and it must be made of the heaviest-gauge sheet iron you can find. Likewise, its cover must be ample: e.g., a fourteen-inch wok should have a twelve- or thirteen-inch cover, in order to leave the maxi-

mum amount of room inside. (Anything larger than a sixteen-inch wok generally takes up too much room on the average stove top; anything smaller tends to cramp your style
when stir-frying and to restrict you when you steam things.)
The only exception to the rules is the ring in which it sits
over the burner: while it should be large enough in diameter
to fit *around* the burner grid (resting, thus, on the stove top
itself, not the grid), it must be low enough to get the wok as
close as possible to the source of heat. It may be of sheet iron
or aluminum. The cover, on the other hand, will almost always be of aluminum. (The best shape for that, by the way,
has a trapezoidal cross section, not a semicircular one. A good
lid also has a handle like an old-fashioned drawer pull, not a
solid wooden one. The reason for this is that when you become adept at stir-frying, you remove the lid by lifting it
with the blade of the *wok chan,* not with your hand; insula-
tion becomes unnecessary.)

Of course, you also need a *wok chan* and a *siou hok*
(turner and ladle respectively), but they're not a problem.
Places that sell woks always sell the tools. Get the stainless-
steel kind if possible. And if you feel rich, get a perforated
siou hok or a bamboo-handled wire strainer as well, so you'll
be able to fetch food and leave the liquid behind when you
want to.

The wok itself should be of sheet iron, not aluminum.
Aluminum is a bit too good at heat transfer and produces undesirable hot spots. It should also be (even for an electric
stove) of the traditional bowl shape, not flat-bottomed. Only
the round-bottomed kind gives you the guarantee that whatever liquid there is in the pan will gravitate to the hottest
part and thus militate against scorching the food.

With that in hand, however, you have gotten yourself the
most versatile cooking utensil you will ever own. Care for it
as if it were cast iron (plastic-ball scrub, cold-water rinse, and
a little oil on the surface when you put it away) and it will
last as long as you do, which is all any of us can reasonably

ask of anything here below. —In the meanwhile, you get a host of services you never even thought of.

First, it is a stir-fryer, enabling you to cook meats and vegetables without pouring a single bit of goodness down the drain. Nothing escapes but a little steam and a gorgeous bouquet.

Second, it is a boiler. A fourteen-inch wok easily holds three quarts of water, and it holds it over a broad area. Never again will you have to wait for the bottom ends of the spaghetti to soften sufficiently to let the top parts down into the bath: it all goes in at once, and without breakage. Furthermore, the roundness of the wok fits what you boil. Few cuts of beef, and no chickens, have flat bottoms. In a wok all meats sit deeper, in less water, than they do in Western-style pots; and the resultant broth is more concentrated in the bargain.

Third, it is a deep-fryer. If the round bottom was a convenience when it came to boiling, it is a positive money-saver here. Two cups of oil in a flat-bottomed pot is never enough for anything. Two cups in a wok is just fine for quite a bit of chicken or fish; a quart will make French fries for a large family. In addition, a wok that is used frequently for deep frying is a happy wok: its seasoned surface, so often abused by mere water, is refreshed and restored by the emollient bath.

But finally, it is a steamer. Americans, by and large, don't steam many things—mostly, I suppose, because they think they don't have the equipment. But with a sixteen-inch wok, all you need are three chopsticks laid triangularly in the bottom, and you're in business. Behold:

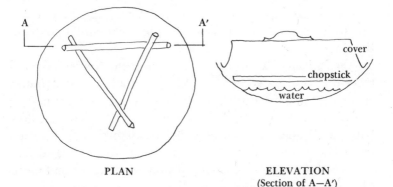

PLAN

ELEVATION
(Section of A—A')

Now, just fill a deep plate with something good to steam, put it on top of the chopsticks, set some water boiling underneath, and let the lid reign over all. . . .

Ah, again!

STEAMED FISH SLICES

☐ Cut a pound of fillet of flounder in bite size pieces. Or, alternatively, slice up a pound of cod, haddock, hake, or what have you. Arrange the pieces tastefully in a large pie plate or other suitable dish that will fit in the wok, and salt discreetly.

Shred into fine julienne three thin slices of fresh ginger, five soaked black Chinese mushrooms, one scallion cut into inch-long pieces. Do the same with a small, thin slice of Smithfield ham. Add these to the following mixture: 1 T. vinegar, 1 T. dark soy sauce, 1 T. peanut oil, a pinch of sugar, and a dash of pepper. Mix well and distribute attractively on top of the fish slices.

Steam for 4 minutes and serve immediately—right from the dish you steamed it in. Garnish with fresh coriander leaves, chopped scallion, or both.   □

The best thing about steaming is that the dish can be prepared hours in advance, tucked in the refrigerator till you need it, and then cooked while you join the crowd for one last sip of whatever it is you're having before dinner. All for the price of a wok.

Just a word about the remaining essential equipment before we pass on to knives.

Mixing bowls, etc. Allow yourself four, preferably oven-proof ones, so they can double their usefulness; but then cheat all you like, using tea cups, cereal dishes, and idle plastic containers. A one-quart measuring cup is probably a necessity, too; but measuring spoons are not. The palm of your hand, coupled with the astonishing accuracy of the trained eye, is all you need. To become perfect, simply do this: the next time you are trapped in somebody's house on a Saturday afternoon and find yourself bored to the medulla with the conversation, select some unsuspecting nine- or ten-year-olds and propose a game. Invite them to fetch the salt box, the sugar bowl, the vanilla extract, Mommy's set of measuring spoons and the bottle of Jamaica rum, and see if they can learn to measure accurately without the spoons. Allow them first to put a level tablespoonful of sugar in the palms of their hands; but then require them to repeat the measurement by eye only. And, of course, join in the game yourself; teaching is the best way to learn. (From time to time, a second or third reassessment of the sight and heft of the accurate measurement may be permitted, but this should not be overdone.)

The rules of the game are as follows:

1. Anyone who measures out sugar with reasonable accuracy gets to eat it.

2. Anyone who measures with gross inaccuracy has to eat ¼ tsp. salt, unless he can measure *that* accurately.

3. The grand champion (¼ tsp., ½ tsp., 1 tsp., 1 T., measured correctly, all in row) gets to eat 1 T. sugar without measuring, plus all the vanilla he wants on it.

4. The originator of the game (you) gets a sip of rum for every correct measurement by anybody, and an extra glassful to celebrate each grand championship. If you play this game with very clever children, it is probably a good idea to set a time limit, or not drive home, as the case may be. In any event, you will return to your adult company either bore-proof or not at all, one afternoon the richer and one important step further from the yawning gates of hell.

Wooden spoons, et al. Let us agree to three only: a long one, a short one, and something flat that will serve as a spatula and for scraping things off the bottoms of pots. Steel spatulas have their uses, but I don't like the sound they make as they scrape tiny bits of metal into the food. A little iron in the diet is harmless enough, maybe even beneficial. But aluminum?

Steel spoons? Oh, all right, even though you already have a wok chan and siou hok. One set only, though: spoon, fork, and pancake turner. A slotted spoon? Dear me. I thought I told you to buy a perforated siou hok. But if you must . . .

Sieves, collanders? Yes, by all means. One of each, with the sieve as large and as fine as possible. But use them, please —especially the collander. When you cook pasta, set the collander over the serving bowl before you drain the pot of spaghetti. Take the curse of coldness off the dish.

Eggbeaters, whisks? One of each, just for the convenience —though two forks and a little labor-intensive application of yourself will do the work. Can opener? All right, provided it's hand powered—but you won't really need it for the few cans you'll be opening in your resurrection as a true cook. Cutting board? Yes, but that goes with the knives. Swivel parer? So does that; but really now. No, you can't have one. If I let you go on like this, we'll end up with my old kitchen and no reform at all. I insist we head for the barn.

Ten years ago, I wrote at length—and with some testiness —on the subject of knives. I am happy to report that since then things have changed for the better in the cutlery department. Not that there aren't plenty of worthless knives on the market—it still takes a search to turn up good ones. But most reliable cookware stores, and all restaurant suppliers, now have good German cutlery; if we were not in the business of simplification and renewal, I could write us up an order that would make them check our credit rating before they filled it.

But since it is precisely that business we are in—the work of doing more with less, of closing off all avenues but the king's highway—I am going to be more highhanded with you here than anywhere else. I shall insist that you leave yourself no escape at all from the discovery of the best. Accordingly, I allow you a mere five items in the knife department, and only two of them knives. For shock value, I reverse my order of exposition, and give you the list first.

one (1) cutting board
one (1) two-sided carborundum stone
one (1) sharpening steel
one (1) Swiss army knife
one (1) Chinese cleaver (*choy doh*)

Please note that your pique, annoyance, disbelief, or even downright anger at this point does not bother me in the least. I have provoked it deliberately. Sooner or later you will thank me.

As to cutting boards, any good, hardwood board will do. Just remember that the largeness/heaviness rule, here as elsewhere, still prevails. Something 18″ × 24″ × 1½″ is by no means too big. An ordinary breadboard, 14″ × 20″ ×

¾", is almost too small. The best thing is a seven-inch-thick slice of the largest seasoned maple log you can find: a diameter of fourteen inches should be considered the absolute minimum.

You object that such items are hard to take out and put away. Of course they are. That is why they are never taken out and put away; they live their whole lives right on the counter, as every true cutting surface does. Stowing them makes about as much sense as stowing a sink or a stove. Even to think of such a thing is to prove you have no conception of what a cutting board is. Therefore, please attend.

A cutting board is the other half of a knife. It is no more an optional or occasional piece of equipment than is the one half of a pair of scissors. It does not exist for the sake of the food—any clean surface will serve for that; it exists for the sake of the knife because

a knife is an extremely fragile thing. I mean, of course, a sharp knife. A dull one is not a knife at all; it is simply a sad reminder that you once had a knife. A true knife has an edge of microscopic fineness and delicacy. It should never come in contact with anything harder than bone; not Formica, not tile, and certainly not stainless steel. Furthermore, even with proper use,

there is no such thing as a permanently sharp knife, any more than there are permanently beautiful gardens, or permanently hot omelets. Perdurability comes only with heaven; here on pilgrimage, there is nothing that can safely be left to fend for itself: not your loves, not your lives, not your liaisons, and certainly not your knives. Accordingly, this brings us to items two and three, the stone and the steel, because

a knife is not an inactive object. It is, in fact, a member of a very busy and popular dance troupe and, as such, must be kept in shape. A knife that never meets a sharpening stone is like a dancer who never eats and never practices: it loses its competence altogether. And a knife without a sharpening steel is like a dancer without a bar: it goes on stage with no warm-up, no honing, no *edge*. Therefore,

a knife is not sharpened from time to time; it is touched up on the steel before every use. You find that excessive? That is only because you have hitherto thought of knives as things with which you have no working or loving relationship. (I was going to say it's because you are mad, which is the same thing, but the soft answer is always better. I shall be patient.) Would you bring flowers into the house and not put them in water? Meat, and not refrigerate it? Lettuce, and store it in the oven? Your love, and never touch her? But you see the point, of course: it is laziness, not hate, that is the great enemy of love. Just stir yourself a bit, therefore; it only hurts at the beginning.

Obviously, you will need to practice a lot before you are good with stone and steel. Acquiring the technique takes time and patience—one does not learn overnight the control necessary to maintain an angle of twelve degrees in either direction. The stone is used only occasionally, for major sharpenings when there are nicks to be removed, or after long neglect. The steel is used every time you pick up the knife. If you are right-handed, you hold the steel in your left hand and the knife in your right and stroke the blade on the steel, first over it, then under it, with alternating strokes. The edge of the knife is, of course, drawn toward you rather than away from you, for maximum effectiveness. Perhaps the best thing, however, is to find yourself a good teacher—watch a professional butcher, who will show you not only the method but also the insouciant ease with which it can be done once it becomes second nature.

You say you have no such mentor, that all your butchers are hidden in deep recesses behind the freezer case? Then come and visit me someday, bringing a bottle of good Calvados or a case of California chablis—gallons, please—to cover the cost of tuition. I guarantee you will be able to shave with the edges you learn to produce. And even if you flunk the course, we'll still have the chablis to make up for the failure.

Which brings us, at last, to the knives themselves.

Get a Swiss army knife. Good ones are expensive—more so every year, it seems—but don't run out and buy a mere paring knife unless you're absolutely broke. The large blade of the Swiss Wonder will do anything a paring knife will do: open clams, peel potatoes, scrape carrots, bone meat. The can opener will get you through the minimal amount of can-opening necessary in your reformed state. And the rest of the admirable pocket workshop it boasts will equip you for any number of other businesses: saw, file, auger, screwdrivers, and wire cutter for home-improvement; scissors for manicure, pedicure, and mustache-trimming; and the corkscrew for catering and the general alleviation of *taedium vitae* wherever you find it. If you object that it bulges in your pocket like a giant dog biscuit, buy a long shoestring and hang it from your belt. Just don't let merely cosmetic considerations keep you from buying the largest one you can afford. And make sure it's Swiss. Anything else is a waste of money, no matter how cheap it is.

But finally, the *choy doh,* or Chinese cleaver. Most people, especially women, find them forbidding at first. Let me begin, therefore, by arousing your interest, and so your hope. After that, no obstacle will seem too great.

1. *It slices.* And I mean *it* slices, not you. All you do is guide it properly; the weight of the instrument itself does nine tenths of the work.

2. *It chops, shreds, dices,* or *chunks* anything; and with practice, it does it *fast.* Like lightning, in fact. Watch a Chinese chef some day.

3. It *bones* chickens, *fillets* and *skins* fish, *trims* cheeses and artichokes, and does almost all the cutting jobs in the kitchen except the paring of round objects (for which you have the Swiss army knife) .

4. It *crushes* and *minces*—garlic, peppercorns, ginger,

spices, shallots, whatever. You just bring the flat of the blade down squarely and resolutely on the ingredient and the job is done.

It all takes practice, of course, but then even Nureyev wasn't born dancing. The best thing to do is watch the experts and try to imitate them; the second best, to get a good elementary Chinese cookbook and follow instructions. All I shall give you here are one or two pointers to get you over the first, hardest hurdles.

A *choy doh* must be heavy enough to do its work. They come in many sizes, ranging from extremely light ones even a child can manage, to four- and five-pound monsters that can dismantle a whole side of pork in short order. The one you choose, if you have never used one before, must be rather larger and heavier than you think, but not heroically so. It is an instrument to be used with respect and care. If all your effort has to go into merely lifting it, your absence of mind about where it's going can easily produce a bit of absent finger.

Still, it really must be heavier than you first think. It will help you to make your selection if I state categorically that the handle of the *choy doh* does not serve the same purpose as the handle of a conventional knife. It is not picked up by the whole hand: only the little finger, ring finger and heel of the hand touch the actual handle; the blade is in between the thumb and the index-and-middle-finger—placed rather well up on it, as a matter of fact. This puts the pressure of your grip on the knife much closer to the center of balance,

and so eliminates most of the knife's leverage against you. A heavier *choy doh,* held properly, will therefore seem lighter in the hand than a light one held as if you were about to commit mayhem with it. *It,* as I said, will do most of the work; all your attention will go, as it should, to the precision with which it does it.

But all this is far too theoretical. Let me get a whole chicken out of the refrigerator and show you the Chinese cleaver in action as the *premier danseur* it is. Attend carefully. I am going to show you how to bone a whole chicken (reverse things if you're left-handed).

1. Set the chicken on the cutting board with its back down and its wings toward you.

2. Touch up the *choy doh* on the steel.

3. Extend the left wing a bit and set the edge of the cleaver a little above the wing joint (so that the detached wing will actually have an extra bit of breast meat on it). Then, using both hands on the cleaver, bear straight down on it with all your weight, right from the shoulders. (Don't worry about where the actual joint is, a sharp cleaver goes through any part of any chicken with one good push.)

4. Repeat step 3 to remove the right wing.

5. Reverse the chicken end for end so that the drumsticks face you.

6. With the *choy doh,* cut through the skin between the legs and the body on each side. (Two clean, light strokes are all you need for this.)

7. Pick up the chicken by the legs (by the knees, actually—and with a good firm grip) and bend the legs downward and outward away from the carcass until the thigh bones break out of the hip joints. (There is no way of writing this sort of direction that does not border on the regrettably familiar or shockingly violent, depending on your sensibilities. The world of eating is a rather rough place. Its savageries are a bit more explicit in butchering, but I'm sure the violations we wreak on lettuces are just as gross in their own way. In any event, there's no way of making a case for vegetarianism out of it.)

8. Put the chicken down on its back again and, with the point of the *choy doh,* cut the legs away from the body as close to the exposed hip joint as possible.

9. If desired, cut the legs in two at the knee joint. Just put the cleaver anywhere near the middle and bear down with both hands. (When you become proficient, you'll do this with a single, one-handed swing of the cleaver. Try that, by all means. While you're working to become proficient, however, keep your other hand out of the way.)

10. Pick up the carcass and pull the skin off the breast.

11. Lay the carcass down on its side and remove the breast facing you: working from the far end, use the point of the cleaver and cut along the upper side of the sternum and breastbone, staying as close to the carcass as possible and leaving behind as little meat as you can. Peel back the meat with your left hand as it comes away and, following the contours of the body, cut the breast away in one piece.

12. Turn the carcass over, reverse it end for end, and repeat step 11 in removing the other breast.

13. Pick up the now denuded carcass, take out the package of giblets, if you haven't done so already, hold the carcass vertically by the tail, and with one careful but decisive stroke, chop it in two. (This cut, obviously, is made *between* the backbone and the sternum and straight down parallel to the spine; if you went *through* the backbone, you'd also go through your left hand.)

14. Chop up the remains of the carcass, neck, etc., ad lib, and make stock (p. 43) if you're ready; or wrap the pieces and freeze them till you are. Never throw them out. If you don't want stock, they make an excellent Chinese dish (see below).

15. Wrap each of the pieces of cut-up chicken in plastic foil and freeze them in a bag. I usually do four chickens at a time this way. Yield: eight filleted breasts; eight wings; eight drumsticks; eight second joints; four quarts of good, strong stock from three of the carcasses (freeze at least some of it in ice-cube trays and store the cubes in a bag); a cup

or so of boiled chicken pickings from the remains in the stockpot (for salad); and one cut-up carcass for the following recipe.

SWEET AND SOUR CHICKEN BONES

☐ The only new wrinkle in this recipe is that the pieces of carcass (one inch square, roughly) are coated with a marinade that has enough cornstarch in it to make it the consistency of very heavy cream, and then deep-fried till they are a good color. They go back into the wok only at the last minute of cooking the dish.

The marinade's proportions are as follows: 1 part soy sauce, 1 part peanut oil, 2 parts sherry, pepper and sugar to taste, and cornstarch sufficient. Start by using one tablespoon for each part and see how you make out.

For the rest, cut one green pepper and 2 rings of pineapple into one-inch squares to match the chicken, cut a carrot into very thin slices crosswise, and mince 2 cloves garlic. Have ready at the stove water, vinegar, dark soy sauce, and sugar.

Put a cup or so of peanut oil in the wok and deep-fry the pieces of marinated chicken carcass to a good color; set aside. Remove the oil from the wok. Add to the wok ½ cup water, ¼ cup vinegar, 2 or 3 T. dark soy sauce, 5 T. sugar (or to taste), and the cut-up pepper, pineapple, carrot, and garlic. Cover and boil for a few minutes.

Correct the seasoning, thicken with cornstarch solution, add the pieces of fried chicken carcass, let them just heat through, and serve promptly over rice.   ☐

It's not as complicated as it looks—only two steps, really —and it also works with deep-fried boned chicken, deep-fried pork cubes, deep-fried shrimp, deep-fried fish, and deep-fried bedroom slippers. But the carcass is a free meal and therefore

beats them all. (You don't, of course, eat the bones themselves; but you eat everything you can get off them. Admittedly, it's not like wolfing down chunks of fillet; this is flavor
enjoyed at leisure. Whoever said all dinners should be bolt-
able?)

VI

DEADLY WEAPONS

efore moving on to the actual ingredients of cookery, I think we need a very short chapter on nonequipment. Renewal and reform, alas, can never be totally positive propositions; we have too many bad habits and unfortunate dependencies for that. Many of the things we have relied on, while often good enough in themselves, have prevented, more than fostered, our development as cooks. Some of them are indeed conveniences; but convenience can be a snare, or even a tyranny. An electric blender, for example, is a useful gadget, but if it brings you to the point of thinking you cannot make shrimp toast without it, it has conned you into believing a lie.

As a first exercise, therefore, make yourself tonight's first course by hand.

SHRIMP TOAST

☐ Shell and devein 1 lb. shrimp and chop it into small pieces. Chop up a small onion and smash a slice of fresh ginger with the flat of the cleaver.

Put all these together on the cutting board and, with the cleaver, chop and blend them until they are a fine pulp.

Pick the mixture up with the cleaver and put it in a

bowl. (I neglected to tell you about this, one of the most useful of all the attributes of the *choy doh*—it is a sovereign scraper and picker-upper. A large French chef's knife—the other of the world's cleverest knives—will do almost anything a *choy doh* can do; but when it comes to carrying-capacity, it slips definitely into second place.)

Add the following to the bowl: ½ tsp. sugar, 1 egg, 1 tsp. salt, 1 T. cornstarch, 1 T. sherry, a turn of black pepper, and a little water, if needed, to give it a spreadable (but not sloppy) consistency.

Stir it all up vigorously and spread the resultant shrimp paste on nine or ten slices of stale bread.

Fry them in deep oil (shrimp side first) to a nice color, cut each piece in quarters, and serve—accompanied by dishes of Chinese mustard, soy sauce with shredded ginger, oyster sauce, hoisin sauce, plum sauce, and rice wine vinegar.   □

There. That wasn't too painful, was it? It's just a matter of slowing you down a bit. And look, no blender to clean up. Just one bowl to wash, one board to wipe, and one cleaver to rinse under the tap. Furthermore, while your forearm may have a little ache in it, the demand for your shrimp toast will soon have it in better shape—for this and many purposes —than it has been in for years. Just be patient. I'm a good teacher.

I remember when I first undertook to study recorder with a professional. I had played for years and was, in fact, better than most recorder players I knew. Do you know what he did to me? He made me play sustained notes with and without vibrato for two weeks. What a comedown! But what a difference in the end!

I shall not be nearly as stern with you, but a little discipline is inescapable at this point. If you're in group one and don't have a lot of gadgetry, conquering the temptation to dash out and buy it will be money in your pocket. If you're in groups two or three, not using it will be good for your soul—and pleasing to your palate as well: all the great cuisines were invented before electricity; with a gas stove, there's nothing (except cold things) you can't make during a power failure.

First, therefore, a list of the good machines I want you to do without for now; then, a list of things you can do without forever.

If you do not have a toasting fork, make one. Let us return to that dismal Saturday afternoon on which you were mired in a company of adults whose dialogue never reached the level even of midget jokes. And let us suppose further that there is not even a single child in sight for you to play games with. What do you do to save the day?

You go to the coat closet and get a wire coat hanger. After wandering around the room a bit, you walk over to your hostess and whisper affectionately in her ear, "Where are the pliers?" When she tells you, you whisper again, "Do

---

NOT NOW

Item	Comments
Electric blender	A *choy doh* (or better yet, two) will do all a blender does. Make this your first break with the energy-intensive culture.
Electric food processor	Ditto, in spades. If it ever comes down in price, you might consider being tempted. As of this writing, it is a mere luxury, no matter what the raving experts say.
Electric mixer	Your hand, wielding a long wooden spoon or a decent eggbeater (both of which I have allowed you), will render it completely dispensable.
Electric dishwasher	Courage, please. No whimpering. If you like, think of your time at the sink as the culinary equivalent of sustained notes. Or chat. Or sing. Or meditate. Or say the Jesus Prayer. Just be grateful you can't go rushing into the next piece of busy meaningfulness.

NOT EVER

Item	Comments
Electric knife sharpener	The correct name for this horror is the Electric Knife Devourer. Only a sworn enemy of knives would ever use one.
Electric knife	It shames my hand even to write the words.
Electric frying pan crock pot slow cooker etc.	Why do you have a stove?
Electric toaster oven	Ditto
Electric toaster	Double ditto. If this makes you furious, it is because you either do not have a gas stove, or have never tasted toast made on a fork over the burner.

you by any chance have *two* pairs—or one pair and an adjustable wrench, or a portable vise, or a pair of vise grips?" An affirmative answer to any of them puts you home free. You seat yourself in the midst and begin.

With the side cutter of the pliers, you snip away the hook and its accompanying twist. Then, with pliers and hand, you straighten the wire to perfection. You rise once more and ask your hostess quietly for a bit of sandpaper. Her husband, who first thought you were propositioning her, has by now concluded you are mad, relaxed his attentions, and gone to fetch himself another beer. You call to him to bring you one, too, have a sip, and sand the wire clean and bright.

Placing the pliers exactly in the middle of the wire, you make two right angled bends, thus:

This makes the top of the handle.

Next, you seize the two wires firmly with the pliers at a point about six inches from the free ends and make four tight twists. Then, leaving the pliers in place and using the other pair of pliers, you make four tight twists in the opposite direction on the other side.

After that, it is simply a matter of giving a nice shape to the tines of the fork, equalizing them if necessary, and sharpening them to perfection with the file of your Swiss army knife.

A little more sandpapering to bring up the finish and you have a toasting fork that will give you a lifetime's worth of toast at no cost at all. You will also have provided your hosts with one of the few pieces of punctuation in the otherwise unmemorable run-on sentence that is their lives: it will go down in their meager history as The Day Old Ernest Freaked Out on a Coat Hanger.

The finished product should look like this:

T. S. Eliot: "These fragments I have shored against my ruins."

VII

A DINNER OF HERBS

I want you to pause for a moment upon the toasting fork. In my mind, it is no mere afternoon's diversion, to be tucked away and forgotten. Rather it is the scepter of the throne of simplification and renewal to which you are the lawful pretender and from which you are now ready to reign. For with my strictures about nonequipment, the austerities in this book are over: from here on it is coronation all the way.

I hear you whispering among yourselves, What is all this coronation nonsense? Here we sit, not a scrap of food in the house except onions, no spices but five, no pots but four, and that Chinese steel salad bowl on the stove, nothing for a knife but an alien hatchet which puts us in jeopardy of life and limb, our rod a rebent coat hanger—and he dares to speak of empire? This is no kingdom; it is hardly even the shank end of a yard sale.

Wrong. It is a kingdom, and one from which all enemies have been banished at that. The unclean spirit of culinary misrule has been cast out; as long as we do not invite it back, we are free to extend our dominion from pole to pole, from the rising of the sun . . .

But enough of metaphor. The subject is comestibles, the edible goodnesses of the world, food in all its sweeping generality—and, *imprimis* and in particular, vegetables in all their astonishing variety.

When God made the world (don't balk, please, at that formulation: the world is a remarkable place and cries out for the compliment of a remarkable cause; that much at least is true), he seems by any account to have lavished his attentions more prolifically on the lower orders than on the higher. There are more kinds of bugs than there are of beasts, and there are no doubt more kinds of vegetation than both of them put together. (There are probably also more minerals than anything else, but apart from salt, the recipe for stone soup, and a decent little boulder to hold down the sauerkraut, rocks *qua* rocks do not enter much into cookery.)

It takes, apparently, a sharpening of the divine focus to ascend the ladder of creation: the genera and species become fewer as he goes up, there being not so many mammals as there are vertebrates, and only one lonely mammal at the top capable of discovering fire and inventing the toasting fork. Nevertheless, the divine purpose in that focusing is never restriction. Rather, it is the eliciting of greater variety still: not just toast, but French toast, shrimp toast, anise toast, zwieback, Holland rusks, English muffins, croutons, and toasted cheese; not a singular *homo coquus* but a noble army, men and boys, the matron and the maid—*quot homines, tot coqui*—crowned with glory and going forth toasting and to toast.

How sad, then, that man—or more accurately, *Homo Americanus*—has allowed himself to try sharpening his creative eye by narrowing his culinary field of vision to peas, potatoes, and steak. What a spurning of the riches of creation to start with only three of the beasts of the field and then to reduce that already meager list to the ox alone. What a refusal of the invitation to abundance offered by the fowls of the air to opt for just two that can't even fly. What a denial, in a land with two and a half salt oceans and five fresh ones, to have a national fixation on nothing but tuna and shrimp. And above all, what a purblind gainsaying of the fecund Word when the little boy in all of us pouts till he gets the carrots out of his peas, and goes into a decline at the thought of an artichoke.

Vegetables, therefore, are the first province of the kingdom of variety to be reconquered. They are, after all, the nearest and richest to hand. The supermarket meat counter is practically desert territory. No wonder people say they wish God would invent another animal: No venison is there, no moose, no elk, no bear, no possum, no rabbit, no hare—not even a package of frozen goat that we might make merry with our friends. But the vegetable counter still vindicates the largesse of the house to which we were born: there, at the price of only moderate adventurousness, are asparagus, artichokes, collards, mustard greens, spinach, Swiss chard, kale, lettuces, escarole, chicory, bean sprouts, hot peppers, sweet peppers, squashes, turnips, beets, eggplant, beans, peas, mushrooms, corn, scallions, leeks, parsnips, radishes, tomatoes, and more—all in addition to onions, garlic, celery, carrots, and parsley. And that's not counting fruit.

Restriction be damned, then. Raised sights are the order of the day. And cheating, too, whenever possible. If you need something you haven't got (say, Chinese dried shrimp to make Szechwan braised eggplant), then by all means get it. It's not even cheating, really: you finally need it for a good reason; necessity absolves you in advance.

Accordingly, just to get the troops moving on the outer marches of the vegetable kingdom, I suggest a raid on sauces for pasta. You notice I did not say spaghetti sauce: the phrase makes me wince. It has been the occasion of strained social situations.

There have been times, at cocktail parties or other one-footed, half-witted functions, when I have been cut out of the herd by some earnest soul and roped with the words: "Oh, you're the gourmet cook. Do you make spaghetti sauce?" I trust you see what a difficult and unfortunate question that is. First of all, it betrays a belief on the part of the questioner that there is a single thing called spaghetti sauce, which of course there is not. That, however, can be written off as mere ignorance. What is more serious is that such ignorance almost always goes hand in hand with the kind of arrogance that flourishes in minds unconfused by any truths save one. You are being addressed by one of the narrow on whom, T. S. Eliot maintains, "assurance sits / As a silk hat on a Bradford millionaire." But last of all, it is almost a certainty that both the ignorance and the arrogance are about to corner you into listening to a recipe which involves nine unnecessary steps, has one all-important ingredient no one else ever thought of, and probably calls for either canned soup or soy sauce.

When I am asked such a question, therefore, I simply say yes, and hope the nightmare will go away. But in my mind, I weep. Why do otherwise passable intellects allow themselves so many unexamined assumptions when it comes to cooking? Why, first of all, do they so blithely eliminate all pasta but spaghetti? Why not sauces for ziti, for occhi di lupo, for fettucine, for fusili, for rotelle, for mostaccioli, for tubetini, for ditalini, for capelli d'angeli, for . . . ? Second, why must it always be red? Why not brown like stracotto; why not green like pesto Genovese? Why not white like sauce Alfredo, why not pale yellow like carbonara? But, finally, why do they invariably assume it's made with meat? Why do vegetable sauces blow all the circuit breakers of their minds?

If, in desperation, I am ever forced into giving a recipe as a riposte to their low thrust, I always give the one below. They take it, of course, as either a put-down or a piece of idiocy, and they usually leave both me and it alone forever. In fact, though, it is the best and simplest of all the vegetable sauces for pasta, and I give it to you in high seriousness to treasure and to use.

TOMATO SAUCE

☐ Open a can of tomatoes, put the contents in a saucepan, chop them up a bit with a wooden spoon, and boil them down to about half their original volume, stirring occasionally.

Turn off the fire, stir in several generous lumps of butter, and season judiciously with salt and pepper.   ☐

That's it, believe it or not. As a sauce in its own right; as a sauce to be sprinkled at the table with fresh basil or parsley and good cheese; as a base for other sauces—and as a sovereign pizza sauce—it is unbeatable. Use peeled fresh tomatoes if you like, but only in season. Just remember that if I ever say Tomato Sauce in this book, this sauce is the one I mean.

On then, to vegetable sauces for pasta.

PARSLEY SAUCE

☐ Melt 1 cup butter in a saucepan, add a minced clove of garlic, and simmer until the garlic is golden brown. Pour over hot drained pasta (vermicelli, perhaps?), mix, add 1 cup chopped fresh parsley and ½ cup good grated Parmesan cheese. Mix once more and serve.   ☐

AGLIO E OLIO

☐ Heat 1 cup olive oil in a saucepan, add 6 cloves of garlic, minced, and simmer until the garlic is a light golden brown. Stir in a generous handful of chopped parsley, add a good pinch of oregano, heat through, and serve with hot drained pasta (fine linguine?).   ☐

PESTO GENOVESE

☐ Take 1 cup fresh (never dried) basil leaves, 3 to 6 cloves of garlic, ¼ cup pine nuts (or brazil nuts), and ½ cup grated cheese. By one device or another (mortar, blender, much chopping and mashing), reduce these to a smooth paste.

Put the paste in a bowl and gradually beat into it ½ cup olive oil. When it is the consistency of thick mayonnaise, beat in a splash or so of boiling water to smooth it out.

Serve with hot drained pasta (homemade fettucine!). ☐

MUSHROOM SAUCE

☐ Boil ⅛ lb. salt pork for a few minutes, and cut it into tiny dice.

In a saucepan, heat 2 T. olive oil and 4 T. butter, and sauté the salt pork until it is golden brown.

Add 1 lb. mushrooms, cut into chunks (or as you like), and simmer for ten minutes or so.

Add some chicken stock to bring it all to the consistency of a good sauce, a turn or so of black pepper, salt if needed, and bring to a boil again.

At the end, add some heavy cream, check the salt, heat through, and serve with hot drained pasta (homemade noodles, say, cut as long and fine as you can get them).

(A splash of Marsala, Madeira, or sherry, added along with the stock, is not a crime.)   ☐

ROASTED GREEN PEPPER SAUCE

☐ Holding four large green peppers one by one on a long fork (your toasting fork), singe them over a gas flame until they are black all over. Flick off the burnt skin (the small amount which inevitably remains is part of the flavor of the dish). Slice the peppers thin.

Coat the bottom of a pan with a mixture of olive oil and butter and add to it one onion, sliced. Cook until soft and golden.

Add the peppers, simmer till they give up most of their moisture, and add salt and pepper to taste.

Add six tomatoes, peeled and chopped, and simmer until everything is tender and the sauce is reduced to a good consistency. Correct the seasoning and serve with hot drained pasta (why not fusili?).   □

EGGPLANT SAUCE

□ Pare a medium-size eggplant, slice it up, soak it in cold salted water for a while, then rinse it and cut it into cubes.

Heat ½ cup olive oil in a pot, add a small onion, chopped, and a small singed (see recipe above) green pepper, also chopped. Add the eggplant and sauté for a good while until everything is golden.

Add a cup or so of Tomato Sauce (p. 107), salt and pepper to taste, and a pinch of thyme.

Simmer 30 minutes, stirring occasionally. Serve with hot drained pasta (how about ziti?).   □

ZUCCHINI SAUCE

□ Slice 1 lb. small zucchini thin.

Heat ¼ cup butter in a saucepan, add the zucchini, and simmer until soft.

Add some chicken stock and season with lemon juice, salt, pepper, and a few gratings of nutmeg. Add a handful of chopped parsley and simmer until the sauce is a good consistency. Finish with heavy cream, correct the seasoning, and serve with hot drained pasta (homemade broad noodles). ☐

You have noticed, of course, that one of these vegetable sauces has salt pork in it. I have included the recipe for it deliberately, just to put a respectable distance between us and vegetarianism. For, like most other *isms*, it is a heresy. To be enthralled by the wonder, variety, and succulence of the vegetable creation is to have come upon a great truth; to treat that discovery as the whole truth is to have fallen into grievous error. For that is what heresy is: the failure to be catholic, the refusal to be whole, comprehensive, and universal in our grasp of a subject. The heretic takes a good idea and forces it into being the only idea. He holds his single truth in isolation from all those other truths without which it becomes not only a lie but a dangerous one at that.

At first you might not think so. After all, vegetables are indeed good. Why not make a great fuss over them? The answer to that, of course, makes the distinction: vegetables are good; vegetarianism is wicked. It is only the latter I want to get off the boards. For, like all heresies, it uses the enthusiasm it gathers from its one truth to make war on all the rest. Vegetarianism, as you may have noted, spends a great deal of time on the attack: it thinks of itself as having a mission from God to tell you what bad eating habits you have.

Mostly, though, it is a bore. In order to bolster its perverse and foolish culinary case, it busies itself with facts and figures that are at best half-truths and at worst patently ridiculous. If the vegetarian case were true, the race would have become extinct long before anyone figured out it was pork, possum, and partridge that did us in.

I am aware that there are practicing vegetarians who will repond to such a charge as if it were a personal attack. But it is not. I have lived long enough to know that attacking people is not only useless, but clean contrary to the Gospel of grace without which none of us, right or wrong, is going to make it. If even Jesus, who was sinless, seems to have been ill advised to inveigh so heavily and personally against the Pharisees, it ill behooves the rest of us to risk our shabby track record with *ad hominem* invective. Accordingly, I have nothing to say against vegetarians. We are all sinners; rocks, if thrown at all, should hit *isms* only.

Accordingly, I ask you to note only that vegetarianism's usual response to the charge that it is ridiculous simply confirms its tiresomeness. It will vehemently deny my overstatement about extinction and proceed straight to some overstatement ten times worse. It will prove that meat-eating causes not the demise of the race but, rather, things far worse: depression, disease, Fascism, Communism, and, for all I know, original sin. This paranoia, however, is frequently tempered by an inconsistency that allows here some butter, there an egg, and now and again a bit of cream. Its scruples about eating meat stem, it claims, from a compassion for the lower orders. Taking life is abhorrent to vegetarianism; it will ingest nothing that has about it the reek of death.

Such pity, though, is the product of a limited imagination. The toothsome world is a harsh and deadly place; a thoroughgoing compassion would make us squeamish right across the board. Nasty things happen to all organic beings when they are heated to 212°. No matter what you are—boy, bull, bluefish, beansprout, or buckwheat—cooking boils the water in you, explodes your cell walls, coagulates your albumen, and makes a general and irreversible mess of your plans for the season. When vegetarianism preaches pity for peas and love for lettuces, it will be time enough to hear it out as a philosophy.

Nevertheless, despite the vehemence of its objection to the fact that it takes life to support life—that by the Love that made us, we all, late or soon, lay down our lives for our friends—it remains a pale philosophy. And it spreads its paleness to everything it touches: to the fauna who allow themselves to be guided by it; to the flora whom it forces to bear the full burden of nourishment without so much as a piece of ham fat to lend a helping hand; but above all to the recipes it concocts to further its dimmed and dimming program.

Not that there aren't some marvelous, totally vegetable confections (I have given you two, quite by accident: Aglio e Olio and Pesto Genovese) ; and not that eating nothing but vegetables can't be salutary (I have cooked my way through a Greek Lent with fun and profit—and with no cheating). It's just that the universalizing of limitation, which vegetarianism insists upon, is as insufferable as it is unnecessary. Anyone who has even halfway well-behaved insides, and who eats moderately and exercises regularly (which is to say, any human being who bothers to act like a human being), can have his butter, cream, and salt pork and be the better for it.

For the world is a tissue of interconnections, an ecological whole, a happy succession of symposia, symbrosia, and all-night bashes. It is a City that thrives on the interchanges of its members. Hence my conclusion: to settle for recipes that lock away in a ghetto a good half of its citizens is simply an outrage. My own formulas, therefore—and especially my vegetable ones—will for the most part be uncompromisingly catholic: a bit of ground pork in the dry-fried string beans, a few dried shrimp in the eggplant, a ham bone in the lentil soup, all to prove the coinherences that turn the world into the loving convivium it is.

Vegetarianism, good night.

There is, however, one more declination from the truth —one more temptation to miss the divine point—that your proper vegetable love must guard against. God has made us temporal creatures; and he has set us in a congenial world where everything else has its time and place—where there are due seasons, high times, and happy rooms for the keeping of our company with rocks and rills, with raspberries, radishes, and rutabagas.

Unfortunately, this is not always appreciated. Theologians, for example, tend to speak far too much about eternity (of which, obviously, they know nothing), and far too little about time. God, on the other hand, has spent a good many millennia trying to arrange dates and places of assignation with the assorted and consorted apples of his eye. My own impression is that he's trying to tell us something—namely, that he likes seasons and sessions and that he would rather like for us to like them, too.

True enough, the higher orders are a bit less bound than the lower by these parameters of time and place. But we were never meant to be free of them; only free in them and for them. We have our rhythms, too, and our favorite chairs. In the spring, a young man's fancy turns, just as the tomato plant's does, to the Desire that draws the world home. In the dark time of the year, we, right along with the seeds and the squirrels, wait out our discontent until we rise.

What a reversal of the divine will, then—what a contradiction of the Word with his fullnesses of time—to spurn those rhythms in our eating and pretend it is always time for everything. How silly to want strawberries all year long: it is precisely in the vegetable order that we find the clearest sacrament of our temporality. God cares more what it is time *for* than he does what time it is. *Six o'clock in the evening, 10 May 1977* is not, in itself, an important fact; it is not even a real one, actually—only a possible description of something that is. But *asparagus for supper* is a fact, and a glorious time-laden, season-fulfilling one at that. And yet we complain: too much asparagus in May, none in November.

Bosh! Where I live, November is turnips, squashes, cauliflower, Swiss chard, sound apples, and good hard potatoes with no sprouts on them. May is mackerel. Asparagus too, of course, but mostly mackerel: lovely fat ones, bursting with roe and milt, and practically jumping into the boat and onto the stove. Too many mackerel, you say? Wrong. If they are not too many for God, they are not too many for man made in the image of God. Half of the world's great recipes are the result of a loving and inventive response to seasonal glut: mackerel in dill sauce, baked mackerel with shrimp sauce, cold mackerel with mayonnaise, mackerel salad, mackerel Breslin-style, stuffed mackerel, poached milt with black butter and capers, broiled roe with bacon and parsley, charcoal-grilled mackerel with horseradish sauce . . . And asparagus? Steamed, with butter; cold, with sauce vinaigrette; leftover, with Dijon mustard; out of the refrigerator, with mayonnaise; hot, with garlic and black bean; cold again, in a rice salad; cut up, in a cheese omelet; baked, in a frittata . . . Why, between the two, you don't even have time to get ready for June, when the strawberries invite you to go mad with sugar, cream, eggs, cheese, kirsch, and Grand Marnier.

I really must give you two of those asparagus recipes.

RICE SALAD

☐ Empty a jar of *Giardinera* (cold Italian fresh vegetable salad) into a bowl, and add extra olive oil, vinegar, salt, and pepper to stretch the dressing a bit.

Cut up some cold cooked asparagus into bite-size pieces, quarter some ripe cherry tomatoes, and add both to the bowl. Mix and let stand awhile.

When ready, mix all with 2 cups cold cooked rice, correct the seasoning, and serve.

(This molds rather nicely: rinse out a bowl with cold water, pack in the salad, and let it stand till you're ready to turn it out.)   ☐

ASPARAGUS-CHEESE OMELET

☐ Break 4 eggs into a bowl, add a little water, thyme, salt, and pepper, and beat them up with a fork.

Slice some Cheddar cheese thin and cut some cooked asparagus into bite-size pieces.

When you make the omelet, heat some olive oil in the pan first, then add the eggs. When the bottom of the omelet sets, arrange the cheese and asparagus in the eggs, let all cook for a while over low heat, and finish by browning the top under the broiler. Slice in pie-shaped pieces and serve. □

My whole point is: don't avoid the seasonal glut; use it to force yourself to invention, and to the rediscovery of rhythmic roots of your being. The market, to a fair extent, still reflects it; but to a dangerous degree, it tries, increasingly, to flatten it out. I note that I can buy corn on the cob on this bright day in May. But why should I? That is August's surprise, when it goes into the pot only minutes after it came off the stalk. Anything I buy out of season will be all but carsick from the ride up from Florida. And furthermore, it would never be enough; only too much is enough for corn fritters, corn chowder, creamed corn, succotash. . . . But there are times when too much is too much, and that's enough of lists.

Let me give you, in no particular order, a little compendium of recipes that do interesting things with vegetables. Their only unifying principle is the fact that I have cooked them all in recent months—and on an apartment stove—as part of my own renewal.

FRIED POTATOES, GREEK-STYLE

□ Peel and cut up some potatoes as for french fries.

In a bowl, put the juice of ½ lemon, and salt, pepper, garlic powder, and oregano to taste. Add the cut-up potatoes and mix well.

In a skillet, heat a generous coating of olive oil almost to smoking, add the potatoes and fry, turning them frequently to brown (but not blacken) all over. If necessary, lower the heat to cook them through. Serve.   □

DRY-FRIED STRING BEANS

□ Snap the ends off 1 lb. string beans, leaving them whole, unless they are very long. Seed some fresh hot or sweet red peppers and cut them in strips to match the beans. Mix ⅓ lb. ground pork with a little marinade (light soy, peanut oil, sherry, pepper, and a pinch of sugar).

Just 3 notes: First, the beans are fried at a very high temperature for about 8 minutes and stirred constantly. When finished, they should have brown burnt spots all over them, and be just tender. Second, when you cut up the hot peppers, don't rub your eyes with your hands—and when you cook them, don't put your face over the wok. Third, in place of fresh hot peppers, Szechwan chili paste with garlic can be used. If you do, watch the salt.

The actual wok procedure is simple. Fry the beans in several tablespoons of peanut oil as above, adding salt to taste; remove and set aside. Stir-fry the ground pork until it is broken up and takes on a nice color; toward the end add the hot peppers, return the beans to the wok, mix well, and serve.   □

PIPERADE

□ (There are probably a dozen ways to make this one-dish lunch. Here is simply the general idea.)

Heat some olive oil in a skillet and fry up a nice mixture of cut-up onions, garlic, sweet green peppers, tomatoes, salt, and pepper.

Break some eggs into a bowl, add a splash of water, season, and beat them up with a fork.

When the vegetables are done (neither brown nor cooked to mush) turn off the fire and add the eggs, stirring constantly till the whole has the consistency of a good custard.

Serve with freshly baked bread, lots of butter, and good red wine. □

SZECHWAN BRAISED EGGPLANT

□ Cube a medium-size eggplant—and soak the cubes in salted water; soak ¼ cup Chinese dried shrimp in water for 15 minutes; soak 6 to 8 small Chinese dried black mushrooms in hot water for 15 minutes. Dice 4 fresh hot red peppers. Have at hand peanut oil, water, soy sauce, sherry, vinegar, red chili paste, sugar, and salt.

Heat ½ cup peanut oil in the wok until it is very hot. Drain the eggplant and stir-fry it in the oil for 5 minutes. Toward the end, add the drained shrimp. Remove the mixture and set aside.

Heat the wok again, adding a little more oil if necessary. Stir-fry the drained mushrooms and hot peppers for 1 minute. Return the eggplant and shrimp to the wok, and add ½ cup water, 1 T. soy sauce, 2 T. sherry, 1 T. vinegar, 3 to 4 T. chili paste, and sugar and salt to taste.

Cover and cook 5 minutes. Serve.

This is hot. But the remarkable thing about it is that, for all the assertiveness of the seasonings (the peppers are fierce, and the Chinese dried shrimp smell purely and simply awful), the finished dish is supremely eggplanty.

If you can't get the dried shrimp, leave them out—or replace them with some shredded ham. □

PEAS WITH LETTUCE

□ In a saucepan, put several generous lumps of butter, a package of frozen peas, and some broken-up pieces of lettuce (the nearer the heart, the better). Add salt and pepper to taste, and season with one (1) herb.

Cover and cook, stirring occasionally, until the peas are just tender. Serve.

Note 1: There is hardly a frozen vegetable that isn't improved if you never let water near it. Between the butter and the moisture already in the vegetable, it will cook perfectly, with no wasted goodness, and no draining at the last minute. All you do at the last minute is cook it for the first time.

Note 2: The single herb. Most people are so used to using herbs in combination, they don't know what individual herbs taste like. Therefore, make this dish often, but with a different herb each time: now savory, now marjoram, now tarragon, now thyme, now bayleaf . . . □

GREENS, BARLEY, AND BEANS

□ Cook some large barley as a vegetable: sauté some chopped onion in lard until it is soft, add some washed barley and some nice stock (3 parts stock to one part barley), and simmer until the barley is tender and the liquid is gone. If the liquid goes too soon, add some more.

Cook some black-eyed peas, or marrow beans, or red kidney beans, or what-have-you, in salted water. (Alternatively, heat up a can of the same.) Drain, and butter generously.

Heat some lard in a wok or deep skillet, soften a little chopped onion or scallion in it, and then wilt a pound or so of greens (collards, turnip greens, mustard greens, beet greens), until they are tender but not mushy. Season with salt, pepper, vinegar, and a pinch of sugar.

Serve in separate bowls, and let people mix their own. □

I really must interrupt my compendium of recipes for a moment. This is an Important Dish. First of all, it is prac-

tically as sound nutritionally as God is good. But since nutrition bores me even more than theology does you, I propose
to skip that aspect of it.

What is more important is that it—and all the thousands
of dishes like it in the world's cuisines—tastes like *food*. I
use the term advisedly: it is my personal equivalent of the
Guide Michelin's three stars or the *New York Times*'s four.
I have no higher praise for any dish or cook, and if you
ever hear it from me, you may rest assured that you will be
at least a sous-chef at the Heavenly Banquet (provided, of
course, that I am, as I hope, on the Dinner Committee and
not hauling coal. Pray for me) .   *rice?? fried potato*

When I make this dish (this dishes? these dish?) I prefer   *p*
to use samp (a kind of whole hominy available only on the   *115*
North Fork of Long Island, east of Riverhead) instead of
barley. But that's another chapter. I also like a little ginger
in the beans. And rather a lot of lard and butter, *passim*.
But best of all, I like to get the necessary cooking grease by
frying unconscionable amounts of diced salt pork to golden
crackling for subsequent sprinkling as a garnish over everything in sight. With a new bottle of Tabasco, or Franks, or
Red Devil, and a good supply of beer . . . Oh, my. "Heaven
can wait" is the phrase that first comes to mind. Or, if you
want me to refine it a bit theologically, "Heaven has got a
pretty hard act to follow." Oh, taste and see . . .

I apologize. The thought of this always tends to make
me go off the rails a bit. Let me recover my composure before
I start thinking of what it's all like swimming in oceans of
pork gravy, with a well-roasted fresh picnic on the side . . .

Something a bit more pedestrian, perhaps:

SWEET AND SOUR FRIED VEGETABLES

☐ Just go back to p. 94 and make the same dish, substi-
tuting a fried vegetable for the fried chicken carcass. Use the

same marinade (or make a tempura batter, if you know how) , dip a vegetable of your choice into it . . .

Which vegetable? You decide. Sliced squash? Cut-up cauliflower? Bean curd? How can you ask questions like this when I have greens, samp, and gravy on my mind? □

I'm sorry. Forgive my pique. Let me try once again.

COLD CUCUMBER SALAD

□ Peel and seed some cucumbers, cut them into 2-in. lengths, and cut them lengthwise into fine slices.

Make matching fine julienne of raw celery and carrot. Drop these into boiling water for 30 seconds or so and drain.

Put everything in a bowl and dress it with salt, pepper, light soy, sesame oil, vinegar, a splash of sherry, and a pinch of sugar.

How much? Oh, come now. Just fool around with it till you . . . □

This *is* embarrassing. Things are getting out of hand. Excuse me, I must run out and look for some collards.

VIII

A LAUNCHING PARTY

Let me apologize once again for the abrupt ending of the last chapter. I am feeling much better now. There were indeed collards—reasonably fresh ones, too—and pork shoulders were 69¢ a pound. It was a lovely nonvegetarian vegetable meal.

Which leaves us, happily, in a position to think about today's lunch. Obviously, there will have to be bread, cold sliced pork, lettuce, and mayonnaise for sandwiches. But since we must not pass so quickly from vegetables to meat, I suggest a soup to round things out. Besides, the bone still has plenty on it. Let's save that and make a soup with no meat at all.

I said there would be no more austerities in this book, and I meant it. But I am going to ask you to concentrate your mind a bit and think as simply as possible for a while. There is a basic philosophy of soup which slips all too easily from sight if you make your soups by following recipes. Indeed, this is true of every dish. Recipes are written after the fact. They are mere—and approximate—records, in an alien medium, of glories that exist properly only in the cooking and the eating of good food. They are to cookery what notation is to music: written suggestions from one artist to another.

The analogy is apt. Extensively detailed recipes are as annoying as baroque compositions with all the ornamentation written out. They hide the *line* of the piece under a welter of shakes, turns, and appoggiaturas that any performer above the level of beginner should be expected to execute according to his own competence and good taste. Modern musical notation systems—and modern recipes—are, if anything, even more annoying: to have to write out the way Joni Mitchell sings words before the beat—and to be forced thus to decide whether she starts the phrase an eighth or a sixteenth note early—is to obscure rather than clarify. Likewise, to give precise measurements for thyme, marjoram, salt, and pepper; to say how much cabbage forms the proper base for a vegetable soup; to imply that even a novice doesn't know how much garlic he likes—or worse, to suggest that it is beneficial to his development as an artist for him to think there is only one amount that is just right—all that is pedagogy of the most unhelpful sort.

It is also a lie on the part of the writer. He did not decide upon ⅛ tsp. thyme and then make the dish; he made the dish and then guessed that something around ⅛ tsp. would do the trick. The only right way to learn to cook is to watch and taste, just as the only right way to sing like Joni Mitchell is to listen to Joni Mitchell.

What I propose to give you here, therefore, is not The Recipe for Vegetable Soup. There is no such thing. I shall not even give you A Recipe for Vegetable Soup. Rather, I shall attempt to give you a stance as a soup maker, a *pou stō,* where your foot may stand in an even place and the congregation sing the praises of your productions. Anything less is short change.

But as I said, it will take a bit of simplification. Let me begin, therefore, as directly as possible.

Proposition 1: *Soup is not flavored water.* To think of soup as water to which something has been done is to make a definition so broad as to be idle. All living things are flavored water—and textured and formed, extrapolated and elated water, too: you and I no less than the lowly onion. However marvelous in itself our aqueous foundation may be, though, we do not shed much light on the world's uniquenesses if we begin to expound them at the one thing all creatures have in common. Accordingly, we need a better definition.

Proposition 2: *A soup is a meeting, a party, a game, arranged for the ingredients by the water.* It is a happy cruise, in which the water functions as the cruise director, making introductions, seeing to it that no one is left moping on the sidelines, keeping the extroverts from spoiling things for the shy, and bringing in the easily tired only when the robust have wilted a bit.

Proposition 3: *A proper soup must therefore stand at as many removes as possible from mere water.* The cruise director is not the cruise; he is only its facilitator. The party on board must be duly grateful to him, but if it's a good cruise, it's one another they'll finally remember. This is true of all soups, even of the ones that try to look as much like water as possible. A rich, clear consommé, for example, will greet the beholder as only one thing: the very soul of beef, chicken, and veal, a quintessential celebration of meat. And a vegetable soup will be a grand costume party with each of the guests busy doing his own peculiar best.

Proposition 4: *A good soup will therefore contain more ingredients than you think.* Even so plain a sail as lentil soup must have, besides lentils, at least onions and some ham fat to keep the conversation going. And if that is true, a genuinely vegetable soup must have a passenger list like the QE 2 in order to be a happy trip. Accordingly, I am going to insist on a minimum of twenty ingredients in this exercise. (I normally aim for twenty-one, but this is, after all, an attempt at simplification).

Proposition 5: *A soup is not an adjunct to a meal*—any more than a cruise is an adjunct to life. It is an experience in its own right and therefore must stand complete in itself.

Even if it is but one course in a larger meal—lobster bisque, say, rosy with tomato, redolent of shallots, tarragon, fennel, and cognac, rich with butter, laced with heavy cream, and topped with salted whipped cream sprinkled with coral—it must indeed be all that, leaving the imagination of the eater so totally exhausted by its excellence that his surprise at the equal excellence of the *paillard* of beef in Madeira sauce with poached marrow will be more total still. And by how much more must this be true if the soup is to be the entire meal? Our vegetable soup must fall short in nothing. Anything else we eat will be simply an adjunct to *it*.

Proposition 6: *Soup is not made in small quantities.* It may seem at first that this is a practical, rather than theoretical consideration; but it is not. Soups, like cruises, are better if they last awhile. The first making of a soup is like the first round of introductions: it only begins the party; the longer association of the guests make it go. A ferry ride is not the same thing as nine days in the Caribbean. Accordingly, soups, like stews, are the better for having sat awhile; and most of them take very kindly even to an Arctic voyage in the freezer. All of which does indeed have a practical conclusion: Always make enough soup for several meals. The bother of getting the *Amsterdam* away from the dock is the same for a short cruise as for a long one; but the pleasure is greater for two weeks than for a day.

I was going to switch to an architectural analogy for the practicalities of this discussion, using categories like foundation, shoe, studs, plate, roof beam, and so on. But with your indulgence, I think I shall stay on the high seas.

First, then, the ship itself, the platform which, by its strength and seaworthiness, supports the whole floating celebration. As I see its components, they are ten: one major ingredient comparable to the steel of the hull, and nine for welding, riveting, and trim to get it launched.

The major stuff of a vegetable soup is, of course, cabbage: one whole, firm head. (It is this that dictates the eventual size of your soup, nothing else. If you plan a considerable cruise get a big one—and, obviously, a big pot to cook it in—20 quarts, at least.) Cut up the cabbage as you like.

Next, olive oil (this soup is resolutely vegetable: no butter, please). Cover the bottom of the pot with a good layer of it, and heat it up.

Next, onions, garlic, carrots, and celery, all chopped or sliced, whichever, and wilted in the oil without browning. Then, the cabbage, plus thyme, bay leaf, salt, and pepper. (The salt, at this point, must not be thought of in its final role as a member of the party. It serves only a constructional function now, to draw out the flavor of the ingredients thus far employed. Accordingly, use it discreetly.) With that, however, our ship is ready to put to sea.

Therefore it is time to take on board the cruise director. The water goes in next, but only in accordance with the general rules concerning cruise directors: there must be enough of him to get things going and keep them from sticking; but not so much as to overshadow everyone else.

And then, finally, the guests: A varied group is always best, with the wallflowers and weak sisters brought in only after the party is well along. Tomato? Yes, by all means. First thing. Peas? Corn? Well, let's be orderly about this. Some categories, perhaps: Greens, Grains, Roots, and Beans. But alas, we have only seven ingredients to go. It will have to be a mere two of each, if we're to stay under the limit.

Greens: how about a box of frozen collards and a bunch of parsley?

Grains: a handful of barley, perhaps, and two handfuls of macaroni, preferably something thick and chunky like ziti (and added only at the end, just before the soup is turned off: pasta fades early).

Roots: some turnip and some radishes.

Beans: half a can of chickpeas and a box of frozen peas

(You see now, I trust, why my normal minimum is twenty-one ingredients: we have not even gotten to corn and limas, let alone Swiss chard, kale, rice, kidney beans, parsnips, lettuce, spinach, or the all-important second shape of pasta.)
Cook it all as you like, for an hour, more or less, adjusting the water as you go up and the salt as you come down, and you have soup. You need nothing else. Of course, there's no harm in a little fresh bread, butter, and wine—even a roast pork sandwich would not be out of place. Let's have a touch of Dijon mustard on the bread though, along with some mayonnaise. After all, if there's a party on one ship, there should be a party on the other, too.

IX

VEGETABLE LOVE

I want you to pause for a moment and consider the excellence of the soup we produced in the last chapter. With one slight omission, it comprises all the major subdivisions of the vegetable kingdom that are commonly used for cooking. What is missing, of course, is the division Fungi; but there is nothing to stop you from throwing in a handful of mushrooms if you have them, so that can pass. For the rest, you have a gala assemblage: roots (carrots, turnips, radishes, onions, garlic), stems (celery), leaves (cabbage, parsley, collards), juices (olive oil), and even one member who is actually a fruit (the tomato); but in particular, you have seeds, the very springs of life itself—and you have them in the two forms that, by their synergism, unlock the protein in the world of plants: legumes (peas and chickpeas) and grains (barley and wheat), Accordingly, it is beans (briefly) and grains (*in extenso*) that are the subject of this chapter.

I have come as close as I intend to the subject of nutrition. The good cooks of the world—especially the good peasant and bourgeois cooks—have always made dishes which were models of nourishment: Witness the collards, black-eyed peas, and samp that caused the rhapsodic, if untidy, ending of chapter seven, and the minestrone we just made. But they brought forth these confections chiefly because they, and those they ministered to, were also good eaters—people in touch with their bodies.

For when the human body is not abused—neither over-fed to the point where, like a goose, it takes in anything, nor perverted in its tastes by a monochrome diet of burgers and shakes—it finds itself in that happy state where it not only wants what it likes but also likes what it really needs. Without having read a single book on nutrition, it reaches, with unerring instinct, for felicitous combinations of foods.

One example only, to prove the point: the baked-bean sandwich. To the best of my knowledge, I cannot recall ever having seen it on a menu. There may be a diner somewhere off the main drag that features it, but if there is, no trucker has yet told me of it. Furthermore, it is universally un-aligned: every adult I have known (myself included) pro-fesses shocked distaste when a child takes the end of a can of pork and beans and downs them between two slices of over-buttered supermarket bread. But, as always, the child is father to the man: we have all of us forgotten some of the best things we knew. The baked-bean sandwich is a stroke of nutritional genius, not one whit behind any of its more re-spectable counterparts: cassoulet, with all those bread crumbs stirred in; Hoppin' John—black-eyed peas and rice—on New Year's Day in the South; Pasta e Fagioli on Fridays in the Bronx before all the Italians moved on to the suburbs; and Rice and Pigeon Peas seven days a week in the Brooklyn that now is.

Beans, accordingly, form the ligature between vegetables and grains. With them in the mix, we have much of the merit of meat before we even get to the subject of meat. Let me give you a few bean dishes, then, before moving on to the seeds of the grasses. If some of them call for no grain, eat them with good bread on the side (if you're fastidious), or just brazen out your scruples and make the sandwich your body really longs for.

GARBANZOS SALTEADOS

□ Heat some olive oil in the bottom of a skillet and soften some chopped onion and minced garlic in it.

Drain a can of chickpeas and add them to the pan along with a chopped, peeled tomato (canned or fresh), some chopped parsley, and some chopped Spanish sausage (*chorizo*) or chopped ham. (If you have to use ham, add a little paprika, cumin, oregano, and red pepper.) Simmer briefly.

Salt to taste, and serve hot, lukewarm, or cold.   □

BEANS BRETONNE

□ Soak some dried white beans (pea beans, great northern beans, marrow beans, or limas) overnight and cook them until tender in salted water. (Alternatively, boil them for a minute, let them sit for an hour, and then cook them. Even more alternatively, open a can of plain cooked beans.)

Drain the cooked beans and put them in a buttered baking dish. Add the following: chopped onion, minced garlic, tomato puree (or stewed tomatoes, strained), some chicken stock, some pureed pimientos, some more butter, and salt to taste.

Bake at 300°, covered, until the liquid is nearly absorbed by the beans.

Amounts? Be guided by the last direction: you're not supposed to end up with soup. If you're worried about the beans getting too dry, add some more of any of the liquid ingredients—up to and including the cooking water you drained off the beans at the beginning.   □

MOROS Y CRISTIANOS

☐ Soak some dried black beans (*not* the Chinese kind) overnight and cook them until tender in salted water.

Heat some lard in a Dutch oven or deep skillet and add to it a *soffrito* or *mirepoix* made of the following: onion, garlic, celery, carrot, parsley, and chorizo or ham—all very finely chopped or ground. Season with salt, pepper, oregano, and cumin and simmer until all is soft.

Drain the beans, reserving the cooking water, and add them to the pot. Add enough of the cooking water to make a rather soupy mixture and cook slowly, covered, for an hour or more, adding cooking water as needed till the whole dish is the consistency of latex house paint with little lumps in it. (With the right directions, you see, it is quite unnecessary to give precise amounts.)

So much for the *Moros*, the Moorish villains of this two-part dish. Now for the Cristianos, the good guys in their white suits.

Make a potful of long-grain rice as on p. 13, but before you add the water, cook the washed, drained rice (without browning) for a while in a little lard. Then add water and cook as usual.

You notice, I presume, that this dish reflects the race's penchant for presenting evil as more interesting than good. It has undesirable theological overtones, but since even Scripture gives the devil the best lines, that can probably be taken in stride.

Serve these two enemies from separate bowls onto opposite sides of each plate, and let the eater reconcile them any way he likes. ☐

For all the wonder of their being, however, it remains true, with only minor exceptions, that when you've seen one bean, you have to a large degree had the whole tour: a few variations in color and shape, but not much else to report. Except, of course, the *report* itself. It is the adjunct and derivative properties of the bean—ranging, as they do, not only from the nutritive to the distensive but from the hilarious to the downright coarse—that make it the notable and so often noted comestible it is.

Still, for all their unconcealable talents, beans, as some sage once remarked, is just beans. A Bean Cookbook is probably not one of the things a wise man would set his hand to. Too much low humor hanging around, and practically no poetry at all. You can get away with a lot by poetic license: "Thine alabaster cities gleam / Undimmed by human tears" —to cite a splendid example the mind's ability to gild even places like Hoboken, N.J. But amber waves of *beans?*

The grasses, on the other hand, constitute one of the honest-to-God great subjects of all time. "Amber waves of grain" fairly leaps to the lips; "a land of corn and wine" is the Scriptures' shorthand for heaven on earth. Grains form the staff of life, and the mere listing of them is music in itself: wheat and rye, rice and barley, millet, maize, and oats —and even kasha, rung in honorarily as buckwheat.

Before proceeding to the culinary uses of grains, however, there is a problem we must face squarely: the position of the potato in the American diet. Quite frankly, the lowly tuber has become too big for its jacket. It is overserved, for one thing. I am always tempted, when the waiter asks me, "Mashed, baked, or French-fried?" to reply, "Mashed, baked, or French-fried *what?*" But it would do no good. The assumption that every real meal has a potato in it is second nature to us all.

What is worse, though, is that on those rare occasions when we do rise up against the despotism of the potato, we never fully succeed in overthrowing it: We lump all the grains together as mere starch and think of them simply as potatoes in another form. To prove that to yourself, you have only to consider the three commonest cereal products with which you replace the potato in your diet. They are the ones which look most like it: white rice, white bread, and pasta. Why not brown rice, with its extra crunch and fuller taste? Why not corn bread, pumpernickel, or vollkornbrot? And why just spaghetti and elbow macaroni? Why not barley, bulgur, couscous, or wild rice? Well, because they make you feel a little—insecure. You have, by imperceptible degrees, become hooked on potatoes. You get withdrawal symptoms when you think of grains as such for dinner.

And yet, what is there to do about that, other than to break the habit, cold turkey? Renewal is the business we're in, not continued acquiescence in the tyrannies of the tuber. To the barricades, then. And for a paving block to throw the next time you decide to have spaghetti instead of potatoes, I suggest:

POLENTA

☐ Put the spaghetti back in the cupboard and take out the yellow cornmeal.

Cook up some cornmeal mush with water and salt according to the directions on the box.

From this point, you may proceed in several directions. I give you two.

1. Parboil some Italian hot or sweet sausages and drain. Spread the hot mush on a large, flattish oven-proof platter or dish. Press the sausages into the mush in some pleasing pattern (if the platter is round, for example, arrange them like the spokes of a wheel). Do not sink them under the mush, however—just up to their waists, as it were. Then brown the dish under the broiler and serve with Tomato Sauce (p. 107) and grated cheese.

2. Spread the mush on a large platter to a thickness of about 3/8 inch. Cover closely and chill thoroughly in the refrigerator. When you are ready to use it, cut it into dia-

mond-shaped pieces, put them (not touching one another) on a buttered baking sheet, and brown them under the broiler on both sides, brushing occasionally with a little extra butter. Pile them on a platter, pour over some Tomato Sauce, sprinkle with cheese, and serve.   □

There. One more blow for freedom.

But by way of encouraging you even further to mend your ways and eat a greater variety of grains, let me point out just one more glaring idiocy in the common American diet: we eat beef to an excess bordering on fixation, if not irresponsibility. Our cookery has stalled at the stalled ox. And yet, how often do we ask what the ox eats? Well, I shall tell you, even if it is shame. Those fat Kansas City steers eat grain. And, not being noted for their efficiency in converting plant protein into animal tissue, they use up rather more of it than is seemly in a world half-full of starving people. (They are also rather slow in the reproduction department: The cow's udder may have four teats, but no one has yet succeeded in talking her insides into anything better than single pregnancies.)

Accordingly, if you have even a smitch of red-blooded American distaste for inefficient middlemen, I suggest you make yourself a promise to do your bit to cut them down to size. Convert some protein on your own, direct: eat more grain at home. Besides, it is the absence of whole grains, with their beneficial fiber, that has made our diet so productive of boring conversations about bowels. Who ever heard of a constipated cow? Eat grain, then. You have nothing to lose but your frown.

Grains are a large subject, however. I propose that we make a simple division to expedite their consideration: grains as such, and grains as bread—with any derivative confections tucked in wherever they fit best. That way nothing important will be lost, but the exegetical apparatus will be kept firmly in the back seat.

And where better to begin than at the most comestible of all grains—the very eatage of frumentaceousness—rice? I have already given you two recipes that will serve as a foundation (plain white rice, p. 13; and Gai Fun, p. 46). It's time now to build.

Gai Fun—chicken and rice—should be one of the major dishes in any program of renewal, chiefly because it embodies a principle of great simplicity: the cooking of the major part of the meal in one shot, and in one pot. You will recall that you began it simply by starting out to make plain white rice: washing the rice eleven times, putting it in a pot, and adding water up to the first joint of your middle finger. But then, when the surface water had boiled away, you turned down the flame and placed on top of the rice a pleasing mixture of marinated diced chicken. After twenty minutes of steaming with the cover on, all you had to do was stir it all up and dish it out.

Now, if you will move on from that position, you will discover what an excellent beachhead I have landed you on. The general rule by which to proceed is simply this: you may cook in this fashion anything that will be cooked sufficiently after 20 or 25 minutes' steaming, or less. For openers then,

SAUSAGE AND RICE

☐ Prepare plain white rice as on p. 13.

When the surface water has just about boiled away, put on top of the rice several suitable sausages. Steam, covered, until the rice is done and serve.   ☐

Notice, please, how much variety this gives you with no work at all: each kind of sausage provides you with a distinct and different dish. Just to name a few should be enough to persuade you: regular breakfast sausage; sweet

Italian sausage; hot Italian sausage; chorizo; Chinese sausage *(lop chong)* ; French or Italian blood sausage; bauernwurst; frankfurters or knackwurst; any of the larger mettwursts (cut-up a bit, perhaps, to facilitate the cooking, and to let the juices run down through the rice) —Holsteiner mettwurst, Niersteiner mettwurst, Polish kielbasa, Hungarian kolbos; or any of the French sausages usually served as *saucisson chaud.*

Note too, however, the ease with which this dish can be prepared: the rice can be washed, potted, and watered before breakfast; when you come in at 6:30 in the evening, you just boil off whatever water is left, plop the sausages on top, and have a drink while you make the salad for dinner at 7:00. Furthermore, if you're game for just a little more work in the early morning, some cut-up chicken, or some chopped beef, or shrimp, or scallops, or even cut-up fish can be mixed with their marinade and whatever bits of mushroom, water chestnut, bamboo shoot, or salted turnip you like and left to spend the day in the refrigerator making friends with one another. The only additional rule you need here is that some foods don't even require the full twenty minutes: the beef will get by with four or five, if you like it a bit rare (tenderloin tips, sliced into finger-shaped pieces and marinated, make a rather elegant dish by this method) ; shrimp can go in a bit behind schedule; and scallops and fish slices need no more time than beef.

For a superb closer, though, I give you

CLAMS AND RICE

☐ Prepare plain white rice as on p. 13, but go a little light on the water (to compensate for the juice in the clams) .

Wash some small (littleneck) hard clams and put them in a bowl. Add a respectable quantity of minced garlic, a like amount of minced Chinese salted black beans (rinse them off first), some chopped scallion, some sesame oil (plain or hot) to taste, some sherry and vinegar and sugar and salt to taste (allow for the salt water in the clams).

Bring the rice to a boil and, when the water disappears down the holes, put the contents of the clam bowl on top of the rice and steam, covered, for 20 minutes.

When the rice is done and the clams have opened, mix it all up gently and serve.   □

For the sake of convenience, I am tempted to call these dishes Rice and Whatever. Really though, they deserve something more impressive: I have just gone back and counted the dishes I ticked off in explicating the recipe. There are twenty of them, not counting possible variations in garnish and marinade. If one lonely item in the Szechwanese repertory can have the name General Chiang's Chicken, then this splendid host of dishes must have a name befitting its rank. How about Field Marshal Factotum's Rice? General Chiang probably had only some merely difficult achievement to his credit—like repulsing the Mongolian hordes armed with nothing but two chopsticks and a red-cooked chicken wing; This Supreme Commander, on the other hand, does the impossible with style: he is your Man of the Hour (Thirty Minutes, actually), conquering boredom seven days a week, and on a budget, too.

While we are on the subject of his dishes, though, let me give you five more. Any one of them can keep the potato at bay for a year; taken together, they mash it utterly. For the first then:

CONGEE

□ Rinse ¼ cup raw rice once.

Put it in a pot and add 2 qts. water, 1 T. Chinese dried shrimp, and ½ dried tangerine peel.

Simmer for 4 or 5 hours.   □

A word of explanation. This, obviously, is gruel. Equally obviously, it is dirt cheap. You buy the dried shrimp in a Chinese grocery and store them in a covered jar on the cupboard shelf. They keep for years. You buy dried tangerine peel there too; but you can also make yourself a year's supply next Christmas when the tangerines are in: just remove the skin carefully to that it comes away in two cup-shaped halves, string the pieces with a needle and thread, and hang them on the chandelier for a few weeks. When they are good and dry, store them in a sealed can or jar.

Still more obviously, the gruel you have just produced doesn't taste like much—yet. That is why you serve an assortment of condiments with it: soy sauce, for one thing, added at the table; and sesame oil; and, of course, chopped scallions, coriander leaves, little bits of shredded ham or diced roast pork, or anything else that strikes your fancy. But that is also why there are slightly more ambitious things to do with congee.

BEEF CONGEE

☐ Make congee as above.

Mix into ½ lb. chopped beef a little marinade made of sherry, soy sauce, peanut or sesame oil, a pinch of sugar, and some minced scallion and fresh ginger to taste.

Just before serving the congee, break up the chopped beef mixture into it, simmer for three minutes, and serve with condiments as above.

A beaten egg, stirred in after the fire is off, is always a nice addition.   ☐

CHICKEN CONGEE

☐ Same as above, but marinate 1 boned, diced chicken breast instead, and simmer a little longer.   ☐

FISH CONGEE

☐ Same as above, but not quite.

Slice up ½ lb. raw fish fillets and marinate. Put some of the fish slices and marinade in each serving bowl and, at the stove, pour boiling congee into the bowls.

By the time you get them to the table, the fish will be cooked to perfection. Serve with condiments.   ☐

For the second time in this chapter, I note some furrowing of the brow when I suggest that you cook fish briefly. Let me allay your fears: the boiling congee really does cook the fish. If it makes you feel more secure, take the fish out of the refrigerator and let it come to room temperature before putting it in the bowls. Or heat the bowls. Or both. But none of that is necessary. Far better that you should correct the erroneous philosophy of cooking from which your apprehension stems.

For in your view—and indeed in the view of most Americans—the purpose of cooking is to make things safe to eat. Saying it straight out like that makes it sound a bit ridiculous, but if you are honest with yourself, you will see that it is true. Oh, I know, you will object that you eat raw carrots without a qualm. But you miss my point: It is the foods that you have always eaten cooked that you consider somehow unsafe when they are raw—fish, for example, or beef. In fact, however, everything nonpoisonous is safe to eat raw if it's fresh. The Japanese have their *sashimi,* or raw fish with sauces; the Spanish, their *seviche*—raw fish in lime juice; steak tartare is a commonplace, a bit of raw chopped meat with nothing but salt is a delight; and clams and oysters—well, they are eaten not only raw, but alive.

The purpose of cooking is not to render the dangerous harmless—if food needs that much help, it needs more than cooking. You cook things in order to make them palatable, not edible. Some things, admittedly, are cooked to enable the body to use them more efficiently: raw rice, for example, would not stay with you long enough for your digestive system to break it down. But in all cases, palatability is the safest guide and the first rule: there are no raw rice dishes chiefly because raw rice doesn't taste like much. (If you have not lost your childlike sense of play and wonder, however, I am sure you have, perhaps even recently, chewed up a few grains just for the fun of it—or munched a little uncooked spaghetti to while away the time it takes to get the water boiling.)

Rethink your attitude toward raw food, then. Well-done steak is a crime, even if it is committed in sincerity; overcooked fish should be made a federal offense. It will not, of course, be easy for you to mend your ways: food, along with sex and religion, is a major subject, and like all such preoccupations, it lies so close to the roots of our being that we very easily become—well, peculiar about it. Some people don't like raw sex either. And most of them, when presented with the plain, uncooked Gospel of grace, act as if you're asking them to eat a live snake. Nevertheless, if you're going to be a good cook—or a good anything—you've got to do more than just conjure defensively with threats that aren't there. To the offensive, therefore; keep America's cooking sane: have a plate of oysters for lunch.

Just to steady your nerves, though, here is something overcooked but uncriminal to occupy your mind meanwhile.

PORK CONGEE

☐ Marinate a couple of pork chops overnight, using the same marinade as before, or just sake or sherry and salt.

Simmer these in the congee until well cooked (an hour or so), take them out, cut up the meat in bite-size pieces, return them to the congee, and serve with condiments.   ☐

For the next major rice dish, we escape, briefly, from China. Asopao is one of the commonest and best of all the dishes in Puerto Rican cookery. If *Damas* and *Caballeros* have replaced *Dames* and *Hommes* as the words of necessity in America's airports, then it is high time this import be allowed to star in relief at your table.

ASOPAO

☐ In a pot, put the following: 1 cut-up raw chicken; 1 large onion, chopped; 2 cloves of garlic, chopped; 1 green pepper, diced; 1 can of tomatoes, chopped; 1 Spanish sausage, chopped (or an equal amount of chopped ham); 1 bay leaf; 1 qt. water; salt, pepper, and oregano to taste. Simmer until the chicken is cooked.

Wash 1 cup short-grain white rice briefly and add it to the pot, cooking until the rice is tender and the whole dish has the consistency of thick soup.

Serve immediately, because it thickens as it stands. (This is not a dish to prepare in advance. However, if tardiness of the part of your guests makes it set up too badly, cut it with some beer and reheat it. No one keeps a good cook down; the beer is a great addition.) ☐

Do you think it is necessary for me to mention that shrimp, squid, beef, pork, veal, lamb, or goat can be cooked this way? You do not? How nice. We are beginning to understand each other.

Back to China, then, for the last of the rice dishes: leftover cooked rice with leftovers. There is a common name for this dish, but if I told it to you now, the habits of a lifetime would cause you to misconceive it completely. Accordingly, I simply file the cooking procedure here, without title.

☐ Heat a little oil in the wok and scramble 1 or 2 eggs (seasoned) in it. Remove and set aside.

Heat a little more oil in the wok, add a sprinkling of salt and a smashed slice of fresh ginger, stir-fry for 10 seconds, and add a big handful of shredded cabbage. Stir-fry for a minute or so.

Add diced leftover meats—roast pork, ham, shrimp, beef, lamb, chicken, whatever—toss in a generous splash of stock or water, and bring to a boil.

Toss on top of this a handful of lettuce, broken up, a chopped scallion, some peas (cooked or frozen), several handfuls of cooked rice, broken up, and the scrambled egg. Cover and let it all steam through for a minute or so.

Mix well, check for salt, and serve.   ☐

Some notes: I usually scramble the egg first and put it back in at the end, but you don't have to. The cabbage should really be bean sprouts. Bamboo shoots and water chestnuts can be added if you have them. As far as meats are concerned, any combination of compatible leftovers will do. At the end, the rice will take up the liquid in the wok: the dish will be moist or dryish as you prefer, depending on how much stock you use to start with.

The name of the dish, of course, is Fried Rice. I just wanted to present it to you in a way that would not trigger two false preconceptions. The first is the notion that fried rice is fried in the Western sense of the word. It is not. In Chinese cookery, it is a *chow,* or stir-fried, dish. Nothing is actually frizzled at all. The second is the idea that it has to have soy sauce in it. It does not. The most elegant version of it, in fact, has none at all—just enough salt to enhance the delicate flavors of the good things that went into it. You can, of course, add soy sauce if you like; but you add it only at the final mixing, and you do so discreetly. The dish should have finesse. It should not look, as it so often does, as if someone poured a whole bottle of brown shoe polish over it.

With those admonitions in mind however, you have a free lunch at home every time there's cold rice in the refrigerator. I just happen to have some, so let me check out my own situation by way of illustration: I find an egg, one plain cooked sausage, two uneaten strips of fried bacon, some frozen peas in a bag, a scallion, and the end of a head of romaine. Oh—and a few scraps of cooked chicken that never made their way into a salad. That does it. If you'll uncork the wine and pour us a drop, we'll have lunch in five minutes.

You'd like some soy sauce? By all means. We have a growing relationship. But if I may, I shall use only a little in the cooking. We'll put the bottle on the table. I promise to wince only inwardly, even if you salt yourself to death.

For the rest of the grains as such, I have only one important direction to give you: think Pilaf. When you cook them, simmer some chopped onion in butter before you put the whatever-it-is (even rice) in the pot. The amount of water you use will of course vary with different grains, and according to your taste: bulgur, barley, and brown rice will take rather more; whole hominy or samp, a lot more. And they will all require longer cooking than white rice. However, they are not as fussy as polished rice and you can always add extra water as you go along: your good sense is the only guide you need. Kasha and couscous? Well, the kind you're likely to run into will come in boxes, complete with directions and even recipes. About them— and about pasta—it is quite unnecessary for me to natter on. Just be sure you cook all of them, often.

I shall, though, give you the secret of cooking wild rice: you don't cook it at all. Instead, you *open* it, overnight, with boiling water.

WILD RICE

☐ Before you go to bed, wash some wild rice briefly, and put it in a large deep bowl.

Boil a generous potful of water and pour it over the rice. Cover and have a good night.

In the morning, drain the rice, put it back in the bowl, boil another potful of water, and repeat the previous step. Cover and go shopping.

After lunch, do it once more, this time adding some salt to the water. Cover, and let stand till dinner. Drain, reheat, and season before serving.   ☐

The wild rice is now ready to use. If you have ever cooked it by other methods, you know how many unopened grains there usually are in a potful of it. This way, you open more of them than by any other procedure; and at the price of wild rice, you want all the flavor and volume you can get. Try it, therefore; you'll never again be tempted to go back to your old ways.

Uses? Just one, and the supreme one at that: as a vegetable.

WILD-RICE PILAF

☐ Simmer some chopped onion in lots of butter until soft and golden. Use a Dutch oven or other large, coverable pot.

Drain the opened wild rice and add it to the pot. Mix well, turn the heat very low and let it steam, stirring occasionally, for half an hour or so. Check for salt and serve. ☐

We have, of course, threshed out only the merest handful of things to do with grain. Still, I shall close with nothing more than a warning: grains are one of the great plain foods of the world; don't hoke them up meaninglessly in the cooking. Wild rice is probably the most abused of all. It's due to the cost, no doubt, but most people seem positively driven to go Escoffier one better and add all sorts of unnecessary trimmings and flavorings. Leave the gorgeous stuff alone. The very most it ever needs are the other good things at the table. Let the eater do his own embellishing; don't preclude his options in the kitchen.

Admittedly, the rest of the grains are never harmed by being prepared with stock instead of water. Barley made with beef broth is barley *in excelsis;* brown rice with chicken stock is an equally happy combination. Allow yourself such excesses freely, then. And for something supremely felicitous, keep in the back of your mind

PORK AND SAMP (or barley)

☐ Slice some raw pork (a couple of filleted chops, for example, or a bit of muscle boned out of the shoulder) into thin pieces.

In a Dutch oven, brown the pieces in some lard until they are a good, rich color. (The secret of this is to add a little water from time to time to stop any spotty burning and dissolve the caramelized juices that stick to the bottom of the pan. After each addition of water, you stir things up, let the water boil off, and continue browning. Three or four shots are usually enough to do the trick.) At the end, brown a nice amount of chopped onion.

Then add the washed grain and sufficient liquid, salt intelligently, and cook till done.   ☐

There are, however, some derivative things to do with plain cooked grain, and as they bear directly on our twin subjects of renewal by simplification and variation by concentration, I would be remiss if I did not give them a few paragraphs.

First among them, of course, is rice pudding. Let me simply set down a few strictures. To begin, I am speaking of this dish as made from cooked rice, and on top of the stove. I am aware that there are hosts of recipes, some of them complicated to a fare-thee-well, for rice pudding baked from scratch. Let them all pass, even if your Aunt Bessie did make one that ended up with a magical layer of custard on top. Rice pudding, to my mind, is not so much a dish as it is a habit. It should require no more thought than doing the dishes.

I shall not even give you a formal recipe. All you do is break up some cooked rice into a pot, add cold milk, a little salt, sugar to taste, and one or two seasonings, then you simmer it for an hour or more, adding more milk as you go to bring it to the consistency you like. If your week has turned out to be longer than your pay check, use evaporated milk and water—and some pronounced seasoning like cardamom; if you're flush, use half and half, with a scraping of nutmeg. A little grated lemon rind is nice with anything; raisins (soaked first in boiling water) should, like vanilla (unless you use a bean), be added only at the end; and cinnamon, for my money, should go only on top of the individual servings.

But, as I said, this is more a way of life than a specific confection, so suit yourself. You object, you say, to heavy desserts? Don't. Simply serve them with light meals. A large green salad with a slab of cheese on the side needs a little starch: leave the bread in the drawer and have your carbohydrates with a good conscience as a finale. Anyway, it's eating between meals that does you in, as you know perfectly well. Just keep your hands out of the cookie jar and no decent meal will give you guilt.

The other leftover grain preparation worthy of note is fried mush. I have already given you something like it in Polenta, but I urge you to go even further: put leftover cooked cornmeal or hominy in a loaf pan, chill it, and fry up a panful of slices anytime you like. Bacon, eggs, and fried mush make just as good a lunch or dinner as they do a breakfast—and under less pressure of time. But for the dish that is mushiest of all, the muchest of all the mushes, you will want to have on hand

SCRAPPLE

☐ In a large pot, simmer lots of chopped onion in lard until it is soft and golden. Add to this the following: some un-smoked pork hocks (whole long pigs feet are even better), salt to taste, plenty of black pepper, red pepper to taste, the herbs of your choice (sage? bay leaf? savory? a pinch of thyme?), and enough water to serve as liquid when you finally make the mush.

Simmer, covered, until the meat falls away from the bone; strain and reserve the stock; pick out all the meat you can find, break it up, and put it back in the stock.

Make mush according to the directions on the cornmeal or hominy box, using the pork stock, with its meat, as liquid.

Chill the mush in loaf pans rinsed out with cold water; slice, flour lightly, and fry.

Extra loaves of cold mush can be wrapped and frozen until needed. ☐

But with grains, as with their Giver, we may speak much, and yet come short. There are yet hid greater things than these be, for we have seen but a few of his works. Wherefore in sum; if you want to feel your oats, get to know your oats; the lot has fallen to you in a good land.

X

THE DAILY TASTE

ookery's commonest use of grain, however, remains what it always was: bakery. Nevertheless, it is not possible, even here, to proceed straight forward. The subject of bread and its making stands as much in need of reformation as any we have touched upon so far. Admittedly, not quite in the same way as did the cooking of grains straight up. There, our renewal consisted of bringing back into play forgotten goodnesses whose place had been usurped by the alien potato. Here the enemy poses as the very thing we always knew: it is supermarket white bread—bread on the rocks, as it were—the foundering hulk of the shipwreck of bread-making, pretending to be a gallant ship to the rescue.

It has been said that original sin is the only Christian doctrine capable of experimental verification. At any rate, it is the one for which the most clues can be found behind every shabbily made clock, in every hollow tree ravaged by the polluting hands of man, and in all our dealings, public and private, friendly or not, with the earth and its inhabitants. But perhaps the most elegant proof of it is the ease with which, in subject after subject, the worst supplants the best.

Certainly there is no place where it is clearer than in the bread department. Everybody knows what good bread is and loves it accordingly. A first-rate bakery is a star in the crown of any neighborhood, and is invariably bragged about as such. Homemade bread, fresh from the oven, hasn't an adverse critic in the world. And yet, what do you find in the American bread drawer? A bag of limp, oversweetened, soft-crusted fluff which, if not handled and stored with the care usually reserved for spindly antique chairs, will collapse under the weight of a child's hand. Indeed it is children (who are most often given as the reason for its purchase) who have discovered the best of all possible uses for it: they tear off the crust and make gummy pellets to throw at their siblings when no one's watching.

For all its insubstantiality, though, we go right on buying it, hoping, as we so often have since the Fall, that a creature of air and darkness can lend our lives a solidity they do not have. We have more sense, of course, than to act very strongly on that hope, by and large, we don't eat much of the nonstuff. We use it as a base for the occasional fluffernutter snack, or as a kind of edible napkin to keep the mustard in the process-cheese sandwich off the fingers. But as everyone past the age of three knows perfectly well, a tablespoon is better for the first purpose, and two slices of cheese with the mustard in between do nicely for the second. Quite obviously, we lose very little love on the bread itself. We certainly don't eat it with our meals.

You object. You say that bread is filling and, since you are watching your weight, you find no place for it in your diet. I think that is false, and for two reasons. The first is that, far from being filling, the stuff Americans commonly buy is hardly even ingestible, let alone likable. I am sure, however, that if you were offered the heel of a freshly baked loaf with your dinner you would revise your regimen on the spot. After all, the mere hope that the napkin-shrouded basket on the restaurant table might contain warm, honest bread leads you again and again to half fill yourself with cold freebees before the twenty-dollar meal even begins. The restaurateur, you see, knows you better than you know yourself: he has his waiters serve the rolls with silver tongs, not to protect themselves (except perhaps from frostbite), but to psych you with the long-forgotten desires of your own better nature.

The second reason is a bit more philosophical and therefore more central to your renewal: you are pettish about what you call filling foods because you have not considered sufficiently the human meaning of the word "filling." You have slipped into the habit of thinking of yourself as a dog, or some other creature who eats chiefly to satisfy his stomach. But of course you are not. For the stomach is the least of all the evaluators of what is good for man to eat. We would not describe food as *stomachable* unless we wanted to give it only the most grudging approval imaginable. A good stomach is by definition uncritical, uncomplaining, and tough. It takes downright poison to get it to say a word. It is the palate to which food looks for compliments. *Palatable* is at least the beginning of a hymn of praise. It takes elation nicely; *very* stomachable sounds like an oxymoron that didn't come off; *very* palatable is praise indeed. And beyond the palatable, of course, there lie the fields of unqualified approval: the *tasty,* the *delicious,* the *scrumptious,* the *delectable,* the *yummy,* the *mmmh,* and the *aaah.*

All of which should prove to you beyond any doubt that the mouth, not the stomach, is the principal organ to be filled. A few mouthfuls of something with real taste will, if you revise your unthinking habits of eating, be more filling than a whole bellyful of mere stuffing. For God has assembled our organs in a way designed to communicate the uniquenesses of our nature. Precisely because we are the highest animal, he has given us, by the positioning of our several parts, certain advices and warnings about how we should regard those things that, while we have them in common with the lower orders, we must hold in a distinctively human way. Man copulates face to face, for example, to remind himself that he is supposed to be making love, not just motions; he eats with his mouth up, not down, to teach himself that it is his head that needs the most filling of all.

Of all the physical properties of food, therefore, it is taste that will always be the most filling because it alone is sufficiently manifold and multiform to engage the mind. There never was a good cook who did not have an intellectual love for food—and there is nothing that can evoke that love better than the making and eating of bread.

I want you, of course, to make bread. But since that is the larger and weightier subject, let me deal first, and briefly, with the eating of it. Only a few bits of advice are necessary. To begin with, make yourself a promise to buy no loaves of white, packaged bread for a respectable period of time. If you do not like dark breads at all, then find yourself a bakery that makes good white bread and buy that—preferably unsliced—for the time of your retreat. Eat it any way you like: cold, warmed, or toasted. Slice it, chunk it, tear it. When it's fresh, eat only the crust, if that pleases you—and always filch the heel on the way home from the bakery. If your bread starts to go stale after a day or two, put it in a dry place and let it go all the way: a paper bag and a rolling pin will keep you in breadcrumbs for the rest of your life. And if you run the rolled-over crumbs in the bag through a sieve, you can have your choice of fine white crumbs, or coarse toasted ones as well.

But it is dark bread you should really try to give preference to. Here the supermarket can be at least somewhat helpful. Admittedly, there are packaged rye and whole-wheat breads that run the pullman loaf a close second when it comes to collapsibility; but even they have more taste. The packaged pumpernickels, however, particularly the kinds with whole kernels of grain in them, usually range from good to excellent. They fill the mouth with texture as well as taste. One piece, toasted and buttered, makes a breakfast you can savor with no jam at all, and one you can get your teeth into in the bargain; a single slice, topped with a mound of chicken salad, gives you a pick-up lunch that can actually be picked up without having it fold over backward. Three slices, cut through as if you were marking them for tic-tac-toe, provide you with no fewer than twenty-seven bases for snacks; one piece, with butter, sugar, and a few raisins, makes a dessert. Open your eyes, then, to the open-face sandwich: try all the dark breads you can find.

It is breadmaking itself, though, that I want to set before you in a more considerable way. Unfortunately, the subject is almost always presented in such detail that people are put off. My first effort here, therefore, will be to give you the most concise instructions possible. Not that there aren't a thousand tricks to the trade: there are. But I am convinced that the best pedagogue always seeks to get the student involved at the earliest possible stage. When I teach theology, I expect my pupils to be theologizing back at me five minutes after the first lecture has started, no matter how dreadful their efforts may be, nor how many blunders I could spare them by seven weeks' worth of warnings. After all, it's *their* theologizing I want—just as it's *your* bread. And when I teach Greek, the first exercise after the alphabet is the memorization of the Lord's Prayer. I do not care a fig if they mispronounce it for a month or fail to understand it for a year: I just want them mouthing Greek from the start. And so, because I want homemade bread in your mouth forthwith, I am going to tell you nothing about the difficulties of making it—you will discover the necessary injunctions as you go, and remember them better for having come upon them in the appropriate context. Besides, every good teacher is a liar. He has to be. If his students ever knew what it cost him to get where he is, they would tune him out the minute he turned himself on.

I tell you therefore, bread is a cinch to make. Here's how.

AMOUNTS

Use 2 cups water, 1 package yeast, 2 tsp. salt, and enough flour (6 or 7 cups) to make it all into a dough, for two loaves of bread. Multiply or divide for more or less.

TECHNIQUE

Yeast: Follow the directions on the yeast envelope, subtracting the water you use to dissolve it from the gross amount of water in the recipe.

Water: Use lukewarm water only.

Mixing: Put the water, salt, and dissolved yeast in a large pot or bowl, and add the flour gradually until you have first a stirrable batter, and finally a not totally unstirrable dough.

Kneading: Put some flour on a clean surface, empty the pot onto it and knead the dough for fifteen minutes. You do not know how to knead? Never mind. Fifteen minutes' worth of any kind of resolute manhandling will do well enough.

First Rising: Clean out the pot, grease it a bit, put the kneaded dough into it, cover it with a damp towel, and let it rise until it doubles in bulk.

Shaping: Turn the dough out of the pot onto a floured surface, cut it into as many pieces as you want loaves, and, working with one piece at a time, pound the gas bubbles out of it and knead, squeeze, roll, or torture it into some nice shape that will fit the pan you propose to bake it in.

Pans: For openers, use iron frying pans, well buttered. A smallish one will make a nice, high, round loaf; a larger one, filled with two fat sausages of dough laid side by side, will make two separable loaves if you rub a little butter where they touch before baking.

Second Rising: Cover the loaves with a damp towel and let them rise until doubled in bulk.

Baking: Heat the oven to 375° and bake forty-five minutes

to an hour. Turn the loaves out of the pan and cool them on something that will let the air circulate around them.

Serving: Slice (or break), butter, and eat.

The whole process, unless your house is bone-chillingly cold, should take about four hours. It can be shortened a bit by cutting the time of the second rising down to ten minutes and then putting the pan of loaves into a cold oven with a pan of boiling water on the bottom and turning the oven to 375° right after that. This produces what James Beard calls Cuban Bread. It has a lovely hard crust but a somewhat heavier texture, or crumb, as bakers call it. (I cribbed this recipe from him—without acknowledgment—in an earlier book and got so many compliments for it that my conscience has bothered me for years. So there. I am an honest man again.)

Obviously, breadmaking is not something you do before going to work, unless you like getting up at 3:30 A.M. Nor is it something you do after supper, unless . . . But since most of the requisite four hours is spent waiting for the dough to do its own thing, you can spend the not inconsiderable intervals shopping or doing odd jobs around the house. Therefore I suggest you think of Saturdays or Sundays as the time for baking bread. If there are not too many in your household, a small fit of baking every other weekend should keep you in white bread without any trips to the store at all.

How do you keep it? As soon as it's cool, seal the surplus loaves closely in plastic bags and freeze them. How do you use frozen bread? Just cut off the chunk you want, put it in a paper bag, heat it in the oven, and slice it at the table; toast, of course, is no problem at all. You are, accordingly, in the bread business: the only thing you have to do is make it a habit instead of a novelty, and you will find yourself one vast, important step nearer the real roots of your being.

For beyond the manifold benefits you reap in the making of bread—the satisfaction of confecting something supremely

good all by yourself from start to finish; the entertainment
of working with beings as clever as flour, yeast, and fire; the
blessed mindlessness of the fifteen minutes of kneading; the
magic of the rising; the sense of competence that comes from
discovering over the years all the things you must not do;
the delight in the almost infinite variety of recipes you can
try—there is a deeper consideration still: bread is practically
the closest thing in the world to resurrection.

Once again, I am not making a pitch but simply stating
a fact. It is not only that this book, with its emphasis on renewal, is about resurrection; life itself is resurrection, or
else it isn't life. Oh, I know. We usually say that life is for
living. But that's too fast. People who try to live by such an
undigested maxim find themselves at a loss to deal with the
only thing in life that is guaranteed to happen: they spend
most of their days trying not to run afoul of death. It is they
who have invented the cult of youth, the horrors of middle
age, the fear of the old—and all the glibnesses by which we
deal with them—the Swinging Singles Scene; Male Meno-
pause; Sunset Villages where Senior Citizens get Better, not
Older; and the grandest nonfinale of all, the American Fun-
eral Home Kiss-off in which, without so much as a salami
sandwich, a glass of wine, or a cigar, we are expected to make
believe that nothing happened at all.

But death is not an inexplicable accident that happens
to life; it is the very engine by which life runs. It is by the
deaths of chickens, chicory, and chickpeas that you have lived
until today. And even the life you now have is a perpetual
dying: not only do all your tissues die and rise every seven
years; your loves and your labors do too—frequently much
faster than that, and for reasons good as well as bad. You
cannot do the same job twice in a row without dying a little
to the way you did it the first time; and you certainly cannot
love the same child—or man or woman—two days running
unless you are willing to carry Monday's death with you into
Tuesday's resurrection.

For to live is always to be rising from the dead. To reject death is to reject the only possible soil out of which life can come. That is a universal truth. Indeed, all that Christianity has added to it is an underscoring of its universality. Jesus did not superimpose some odd, additional truth; he simply assured us, by his death and resurrection, that even the one apparent exception to the process turns out to be another proof of the rule.

Unfortunately, however, Christians have not always done too well by that assurance. Perhaps because they were so impressed by it—or perhaps just because they were bone-headed and tin-eared like everybody else—they acted as if their mission was to tell the world that death is negligible. But death is not a nothing. It is the only season ticket there is to life. I said before that Lazarus at the dinner table confuses the troops. Well, the biggest confusion he causes stems from the fact that he knows why he is alive, while they only think they do. In their minds, it is they who are the reason for their sitting thus in company: they drove themselves there, in the Jaguars they bought, with the money they earned, from the successes they had—all of which they now retail to one another over coffee and Drambuie. But in Lazarus's mind, there is only one reason: somebody else's life. They, even in their most depressed moods, consider themselves merely deadish; Lazarus knows he is dead. And they, even at their best, are afraid that the deadishness will do them in; Lazarus, having been utterly done in, can spend his time on happier things.

For he has done the one thing needful: he has confronted the truth—his death—and brought it with him to the party as the bottle from which God pours him the water of life. God doesn't just make life out of life. He started this cosmic party with a world too hot for any life to handle; and, apparently, he will send us all home with a shoulder too cold for anyone to touch. But that is only the way in which he throws the party, not the party itself. The important thing to remember is that it's his party, and if we'd like to enjoy it, it's pretty silly to object to his style, especially since it seems to be the only party around.

That's where bread comes in as the great sacrament of life. Unless the seed had died there would have been no wheat; unless the wheat had been ground, no flour; without the destruction of carbohydrates by the yeast, no rising; without the murder of the yeast by fire, no finished bread; and without the finishing off of the bread by you and me, no accomplished us at all. But the crucial point is that without this whole tissue of deaths at every moment, there simply would be nothing.

Note well "at every moment." Death is not an eventuality that with luck, waits for another day. It is today's cup from which God now insists you drink. If you think that somehow you can choose today not to carry the deaths of your past life and former loves, you are wrong. There is no choice about that: if you rise at all, it will be from those. And it will be from those as perpetually present to you— as carried by you and offered by you to all the others who alone can give you life. The only choice you have is between accepting those deaths or pretending to a life that doesn't exist.

As I've said, this book is about renewal. And though it deals with what are commonly thought of as the lesser things of life, there is no way of touching even them without being dragged all the way to death and resurrection. Whether you are starting up, starting over, or just starting again after a stall, you must not think that you can get into renewal as you get into tennis, antiques, or leather. Resurrection is not something you do with your career. If Lazarus had been busy with his career, he wouldn't have been where he was when Jesus gave him his life.

So, too, with you; and therefore, the end: brazen out those mindless fifteen minutes of kneading and just go as blank as you can. Let them teach you there never was anything to do about your life: that's a gift only your offered death can receive. You are quite safe. As it turns out, the only thing that's certain is the only thing you need. Isn't that nice?

I think I shall not tell you much more about bread. It is not in me to write a bread manual any more than it is to write a sex manual: for either enterprise, my experience has been overly particular and insufficiently general; in both, I find my hands a better guide than my head.

Let me settle simply for giving you four things to do— with bread—when, as it always does, the first freshness passes and you begin to think that what you have is for the birds. That happens, of course, in all departments of life; but since my successes with stale bread seem to outshine my other triumphs over tiredness, I shall confine my advice to that alone. For the first therefore, I offer

GAZPACHO

☐ Break up 3 or 4 thick slices of stale Italian or French bread (or an equivalent amount of stale hard roll or other white bread) in a bowl. Add to it 1 or 2 cloves of garlic, minced, and pour over it a generous amount of good olive oil. Cover everything with cold water to the depth of your thumbnail and let it soak for a couple of hours.

Open a large can of tomatoes, break them up with your fingers, flick the seeds back into the can, and put the tomato meat in the bowl with the soaked bread. Sieve the juice into the bowl, discarding the seeds, and add a chopped onion and a couple of chopped pimientos.

Purée the bread-oil-tomato-etc. mixture in a blender (or, if you lack the nerve to cheat and have become compulsive about my austerity program, rub it through a sieve), adding tomato paste to bring it to a good color, and chill it till needed.

Meanwhile, chop up the following and put them in

separate serving bowls: onion, celery, green pepper, cucumber (all raw), and hard-cooked egg.

When you're ready to serve, season the puréed mixture with salt, pepper, vinegar, and a little dry sherry, and thin it to the desired consistency with cold water or tomato juice.

Dish up the soup and let the guests add the garnishes ad lib.   □

This is, quite simply, the best of all the versions of this classic cold salad soup, and it's the bread's power to absorb the olive oil that makes the difference. Keep the secret up your sleeve, and enjoy.

A second recipe using stale bread is Fondue Celestine. Let me be honest with you. Both the name of this dish —or, more properly, of this *modus vivendi*—and its general outline have been lifted cold from Fannie Farmer. All I have done is planted the seed of its system in the soil of necessity and watched it grow over the years into a great shade tree. Fannie, apparently, was too busy inventing the modern approach to cookery to notice its possibilities; but I am not quite so systematic. In plain English, I have fooled around a lot. In any event, here are the results.

The basic recipe is simple: you make salad sandwiches out of day-old (or worse) bread, layer them with grated cheese in between in a buttered baking dish, drown them in a nice mixture of seasoned milk and eggs (2 eggs to 1 cup milk) and bake in a moderate oven until risen and browned.

What kind of sandwiches? Well, Fannie was fussy; she suggested lobster salad, with the crusts cut off the bread. That was elegant, if expensive, and I made it only once— back in the days when lobsters still made house calls. I did learn one thing from the experience though: if you ever do cut the crusts off bread, don't throw them out. Simply dice them up on the spot, put them in a plastic bag, and toss them in the freezer. That way you always have the makings of croutons, poultry stuffing and Apple Brown Betty on hand—

not to mention soft bread crumbs if you rub them a bit between the palms of your hands before using. (One further extension of this trick: keep a similar scrap bag in your freezer for raw vegetable trimmings. Put into it all the things you can use when you make stock—onion peelings, carrot ends, celery leaves, parsley stems. You will be ready, at the drop of a chicken carcass, to put on the pot. Just run a cleaver through some of it a few times, add a little garlic and ginger, a few herbs, and anything else you like, and the soup will practically have made itself.)

Fillings for the sandwiches? Ham salad; roast beef salad; roast pork salad; lamb salad. You do not know how to make these, you say? Nonsense. Of course you do. You cut up the meat, mix it with mayonnaise and diced celery, and season it, beginning with salt, pepper, and mustard, and going on as long as you please with cayenne, Worcestershire, chopped pickle, chopped capers, chopped parsley, or whatever—stopping short, though, of the culinary equivalent of the décor in a George Price cartoon.

More fillings? Chicken salad; turkey salad; duck salad; leftover-hamburger salad; steak salad; egg salad; leftover-fish salad—all made roughly the same way, with such variations as your taste tempts or your desperation demands. The result? A perfect one-dish meal that needs only a salad and a piece of fruit to round it out. And, moreover, one that can be prepared and assembled hours in advance and popped in the oven when you get around to it.

But that does not exhaust the possibilities of this dish: with minor alterations, it becomes a sovereign dessert. You make jam or jelly sandwiches (with plenty of butter, please, and with the crusts off, if you like a little finesse), layer them in a buttered baking dish (no cheese in between this time; but a little sprinkling of spirits will work wonders), pour on an egg-and-milk mixture (seasoned, however, with a pinch of salt and some sugar and vanilla, or whatever, to taste), and bake as before. I usually serve it hot with extra jam at the table, but it's perfectly acceptable cool; so suit yourself. The main thing is that it is capable of almost endless variation. Let me do nothing more than get you started in an orderly way.

DESSERT VARIATIONS ON FONDUE CELESTINE

In the Sandwiches	Sprinkled between the Layers	In the Egg/Milk/ Sugar Mixture
Raspberry jam	Ground cardamom	Grand Marnier
Orange marmalade	Scotch	Scotch perhaps? or vanilla?
Apricot preserves	Jamaica rum	Cognac?
Almond paste	Raspberry jam	Almond extract
Currant jelly	Cognac	Vanilla
Apple butter	Cinnamon, Nutmeg	Vanilla
Strawberry jam	Curaçao?	Cognac? Vanilla
Lingonberry pre- serves	Ground cardamom	Almond extract
Pineapple pre- serves	Chopped walnuts	Jamaica rum

But you see what I mean. You will, of course, come up with some rather odd fruits if you tend this tree long enough. However, since not one of them will ever be inedible or even unpalatable, I have no qualms about advising you to do just anything that comes into your head. This dish is like resurrection: you start with dead bread; but once that's accepted, it's all life from there on out.

EKMEK KHADAYEEF (BREAD PASTRY)

☐ Cut some stale bread into slices and then into strips the width of two fingers. Dry these in a slow oven until they are hard and golden rusks. (Alternatively, buy zwieback or Holland rusks.)

Boil up sugar syrup—equal parts of sugar and water,

cooked for 5 minutes. (I can't give you an exact quantity. Just guess. There should be enough syrup to come up to the tops of the rusks in the baking dish.)

Take the syrup off the fire and add honey, cinnamon, and lemon juice to taste.

Butter a flat baking dish liberally, put the rusks into it close together in one layer, pour over the syrup, and bake in a moderate oven until the syrup is mostly gone. Cool, cut into squares, and serve with Khaimak.   □

KHAIMAK (CLOTTED CREAM)

□ Put a pint of heavy cream in a deep saucepan and boil it down by a little more than half.

Season to taste with a pinch of salt and some sugar (you won't need much, given the sweetness of the bread pastry above), pour it into a flat dish, chill it thoroughly, and cut it into cubes. Serve a cube on top of each square of the Khadayeef.   □

HOT APPLE CHARLOTTE

□ Cook up a nice coarse applesauce, good and sweet, seasoned only with vanilla. Cool.

Take a whole loaf of day-old (or older) bread, and trim off the crust. Slice it lengthwise into ⅜-in.-thick slabs.

Select a 1½-qt. saucepan and, from the largest of the slabs of bread, cut two circular pieces that will fit into the bottom of the pot. Fry one of these in butter until it is a light golden brown on both sides and put it in the bottom of the pot. Cut the remaining slabs of bread into long strips an inch or so wide.

Melt a cup or so of butter. Soak the strips of bread one by one with melted butter and line the pot with them: the lower ends of the strips must lie on top of the piece of fried bread in the bottom; they must come straight up the sides of the pot; they must overlap each other everywhere; and there must be enough extra length at the upper ends to flop over on top of the apple filling.

Put in the apple filling. Flop the ends of the strips on top of it so they overlap. Soak the second circular piece of bread in butter and press it gently on top of the whole.

Bake in a moderate oven for an hour or so until it is all golden brown (put a pan under it; it bubbles over.) When it is done, let it cool for a few minutes, run a spatula around it to make sure the sides are free, and turn it out onto a deepish platter. It will collapse almost immediately, but if you have done your overlapping well, it will look like nothing so much as a gorgeously toasted hangover ice bag, replete with pleats. Serve with hot apricot jam that has been laced with a little Jamaica rum. □

It's a little fussy. But oh, my . . .

XI

THE STALLED OX

e come now at last to the greatest of all the kingdoms in the empire of cookery: to meat, fish, and cheese—to the culinary uses of those fellow creatures who are not only most like us but whom we also like the most. I think I hear a sigh of relief. With arrant vegetarianism banished from your mind, you have been tapping your foot, have you not, waiting for me to get around to real cooking. Well, I am finally there, and I do not fault your impatience. To be honest, I share your prejudice. These exercises with vegetables and grains, however beneficial in intent or even delicious in their outcome, do have about them a slightly forbidding air of uplift. It is high time for us to get into something we, and those we minister to, already have a taste for. Our answers so far to "What's for dinner?" have produced more than enough long looks. "Barley and beans," after all, didn't get us much more than a resigned "Oh?" "Zucchini Sauce," a hardly encouraging, "Hmm. I never had that." We owe ourselves some responses that will evoke an unqualified "Ah!"

And yet, for all the philosophical soundness of the American predilection for such straightforward answers as "Beef" or "Chicken," we do surprisingly poorly when it comes to the practical business of dishing them up. So much so, that Beef has come to mean only Hamburger, Stew, Roast, or

Steak; and Chicken, little more than Fried. Pork, unless it means Ham or Chops, is almost as much a problem as Polenta; Veal has all but vanished; Lamb is a loser; and Innards are so inconceivable as to be out of the question entirely. For a race of admitted carnivores, we are rather finicky about flesh.

Why, you ask? Part of the answer has already been given: the potato may have become a petty tyrant, but the stalled ox has become an absolute sovereign, and a profligate but dull one at that. Read the Sunday papers. The meat companies that advertise their freezer specials are not in business to improve your taste, only to cater to its lowest, and therefore safest, common denominator. Almost without exception, all they offer is half a cow hacked into oversized steaks and undersized roasts, plus hamburger patties and your choice of a little bonus of poultry or pig. They operate on the, to them, financially dependable assumption that when Americans say meat, they mean beef—and beef, moreover, cut and cooked in the most expensive and least interesting ways.

Not that a good steak isn't good. It is, and I am as partial to it as my neighbors. But most steak is not good steak, just as most apples are not first-rate nor most avocados the very thing you had in mind. One of the marks of dereliction in any subject is the replacing of its inevitably numerous criteria of excellence with a single, and usually subsidiary, one. Houses, for example, which are actually dreadful places in which to attempt human life—houses with wretched little kitchens, no dining rooms, and sleeping quarters that inspire nothing, not even sleep—sell because they have large living rooms. The rooms of real daily use get short shrift, because the mere image of a room, and a seldom-used room at that, has become the reigning consideration. Instances multiply everywhere: ovens designed as if cleanability were the main thing; burners that do the cook's job of thinking better than their own work of providing heat; frying pans whose chief virtue is a nonstick lining you daren't get too hot; and, of course, the tender steak.

I trust you see what this last has brought us to: the fillet of beef as the deluxe experience of meat-eating. "Look, Henry, you can cut it with a fork!" "Great steak, Madeleine!" But, with rare—and *rare*—exceptions, it is not. Almost all the other cuts taste more like beef than the tenderloin does: I will take nicely underdone crossrib any day. And almost any other cut gives the cook more room to maneuver. I have eaten ruined fillet so frequently that I long ago lost count of how often; I have yet to have my first experience of spoiled shin. Tenderness indeed! Tenderness as a primary desideratum is not even a good thing in lovers: passion, distinctiveness, brilliance, wit, fidelity, staying power, forgiveness—and that toughest of all attributes, honesty—are the main things. And in meat, taste must come first. Tenderness is the cook's work to bring about, not the thing without which she is at a loss. And yet, such is the poverty of our meat cookery that we go on blithely grilling things that should have been stewed and eating great chunks of meat that would have been better cut into little pieces to start with. It is the oldest tale in the world: train your sights on something other than the chief consideration, and you lose not only the main thing but even the something other at which you aimed. You don't shoot a deer in the antlers.

Accordingly, if we are to escape from the present high-priced poverty of our meat cookery, we shall have to do more than break the beef bind we are in. The steak syndrome cannot be shaken by some mere resolve to cook other kinds of meat: roast lamb is not exactly the quantum leap we should be aiming for. What we want, of course, is a host of new and different recipes for meat dishes; but what we need most is an entirely revised approach to the cooking and cutting of meat. And since the second is the more fundamental matter, I propose to deal with that first of all.

The reforming principle I am going to urge upon you is

a simple one: for the time of your renewal, I want you to cook no piece of meat whole. That will mean no roasted joints, no great muscular hunks stewing in the pot, no slabs of steak, and above all, no entire beasts of any kind—with, of course, minor and delectable exceptions of our own choosing. The grand paradigm of this approach has already been given: the directions on pp. 92–93 for the boning and cutting up of whole chickens. But that was only a start. When any cut of meat drops below 69¢ a pound (or 59¢, if you want to be thoroughgoing), you will buy the largest practicable piece of it, cut it at home into ½- to ¾-lb. portions, and freeze them for future use in recipes that either I or your own researches will suggest.

The advantages of this method are quite plain. First, economy. We eat meat to excess in every way: excess of quantity with regard to the amounts we cook; and excess of sameness in the recipes we use. And that is expensive. If you want a good steak, you are always tempted to put back the chuck and buy the sirloin. If you want to eat less, you are forced to pay the butcher an additional price—sometimes a very large additional price—to cut your meat down to size. This way, however, all your chicken parts come in at 39¢ to 49¢ a pound, all your beef meals at the price of chuck, and all your preparations of pork at nothing more than the cost of a shoulder.

But it is the gain in variety that is the largest benefit. Your chuck steak, if it is the biggest and thickest you can find, will provide you with no less than four dishes prepared from the chunks of raw lean meat you bone out of it—not to mention the ground meat you make from the trimmings, and the eventual beef stock you manufacture every fourth steak or so from the bones and fat you providently freeze as you go along. Let me give you a sample listing. From the chunks: one meal of Beef and Rice (an analogy with Gai Fun, p. 46); one of Beef with Broccoli (p. 179); one of Beef with Pepper, Onion, and Tomatoes (p. 178); and, from the

largest piece, one batch of lovely, buttery Stracotto (p. 169),
which will serve four as a sauce for pasta, or six as a filling
for ravioli. And, from the chopped-up trimmings, a small
Steamed Meat Loaf, (p. 177).

Chickens? You are even less limited. Buy four and bone
out all but one of them. That will give you three two-
person meals of boned chicken breast preparations—let us
say, Chicken with Rice (Gai Fun, p. 46); Chicken with
Asparagus (p. 53); and Chicken with Almonds (p. 204);
two more like-sized meals made with three boned-out second
joints each—Chicken with Peanuts (p. 61), for example,
and Chicken with Brown Bean Sauce (p. 203); one dish of
six fried drumsticks, fixed any way you like them; six Red-
cooked Chicken Wings (p. 189), to be eaten hot or cold;
one small batch of Chopped Chicken Liver or, if you wait
until you have processed eight chickens, one Chicken-Liver
Sauce (p. 173) for four; and depending on what you do
with the fourth, whole chicken (you see, I am not a mere
purist), one of the following: a Spatchcocked Chicken, to
remind you of the old days; a Spatchcocked Chicken with
Red Sauce (p. 42); or Hacked Chicken (p. 196) for a
party, with a Chicken Skin and Cucumber Salad (p. 197)
to boot. And all of that, without even counting the stock
(p. 43) or the Sweet and Sour Chicken Bones (p. 94) or
both.

And pork? Two good-size shoulders should give you at
least six nice billets of lean meat for Pork and Oyster Sauce
(p. 201), Moo Shee Pork (p. 202), and Pork and Pickled
Mustard Cabbage (p. 201), plus three pieces of Chinese
Roast Pork (p. 194), for Fried Rice (p. 141), Yat Gaw
Mein, and Cold Lo Mein (p. 195). They will also provide
you with enough ground pork for Dry-Fried String Beans
(p. 116), Pearl Balls (p. 177), and a decent amount of
homemade Breakfast Sausage (p. 185), or Chorizo (p. 186).
You get pork stock from the bone, skin, and fat, of course;
but if you're overloaded with white stock and your amateur

boning has left rather a lot of meat behind, you might consider making up a small batch of Scrapple (p. 146) instead, using only the leavings you have on hand.

If I have made my point, let me say only one word about the actual business of boning: relax. It's your meat, and there isn't a scrap of it you're not going to use somehow. If you leave more on the bone than a professional butcher does, your stock will be the richer for it, or your Scrapple the tastier. If you are less than deft at following the divisions between the muscles and get only two fillets of meat where an expert might get four, rejoice nonetheless: so much the better for your supply of ground beef or pork sausage. Of course, if you can manage to take a lesson or two from somebody who knows what she's doing, by all means seize the opportunity—mastery is always a satisfaction. But even if there is nothing more for it than simply to barge in on the subject and hack away, by all means do so. You will either learn or give up. Without the chance to give up, though, you will never find out if you could have learned.

One last word about equipment: you already have it if you've done as you've been told and gotten yourself a chopping board and a Chinese cleaver. If you have a boning knife as well, so much the better; there is everything to be said for tools designed for specific jobs. But it's not necessary. I have boned out shoulders for years with a *choy doh* and hardly even nicked myself; I have bled profusely, however, as a result of filleting myself instead of the pork with a boning knife. Admittedly, a cleaver doesn't do the best job of boning out a whole loin, but then that's a cut higher in price too, so we needn't worry about it now. The only essential thing is that, whatever knife you use, it must be sharp. There is no way of overstating this. No one can love a dull tool. And since love is the only good reason for doing anything, make yourself a sworn enemy of dullness, wherever it may be. You have nothing to lose but your . . . Alas, though, there is no way of finishing that sentence without your getting the wind up, so I shall let it go. Just be careful, and remember where the Band-Aids are. After all, not much else in life responds to such a simple remedy.

But now to the recipes. I began my section on vegetables with a seven-gun salute to pasta sauces made without meat. Let my first shot here be an answering salvo from the beasts of the field—beginning with one of the richest sauces in the world.

STRACOTTO

☐ Cut into extremely tiny dice a piece of raw lean beef (as near to a pound as possible) —or, if you're boning out chuck steaks, a pound of lean trimmings. Do not use ground beef; it doesn't behave properly in this dish.

Chop very fine some mushrooms (dried ones, soaked, or a large handful of stems) and a medium onion, a medium carrot, a stalk of celery, and a bunch of parsley.

Melt ½ cup butter in a heavy frying pan or Dutch oven and cook the vegetables in it, stirring frequently, until they begin to take on a little color.

Add the diced beef and continue cooking and stirring until the whole is golden and buttery.

Add ½ cup Marsala or Madeira, ½ cup stock (anything, even chicken, will do, and canned bouillon works well) and season with salt, pepper, and grated lemon rind (1 medium lemon, once lightly over the grater, should give you enough).

Bring to a boil, cover, and simmer over the lowest possible fire for 3 to 4 hours. You should finish with a thick, grainy sauce.

Serve with hot drained pasta. (This sauce has a great deal of flavor. Put rather less of it than you think necessary on each helping. The eaters will find that even a small amount outlasts the pasta on their plates. Their first call will always be for a little more spaghetti to correct the inequity.) □

Just to give you something that takes less time, though —and that uses ground beef—here is a quick meat sauce.

PLAIN MEAT SAUCE

□ Put a good layer of olive oil in the bottom of an iron frying pan and heat it.

Add ½ lb. chopped beef and brown it gently for 5 minutes.

Add ½ to 1 cup Tomato Sauce (p. 107) and let it all simmer 5 minutes more. (Alternatively, throw in a small can of tomatoes, or 6 peeled fresh tomatoes, and let them cook down for about 15 minutes, or till you have a nice sauce.)

Season with salt and pepper and, at the last minute, add ½ lb. mozzarella cheese (or Muenster) cut into little cubes.

Serve over hot drained pasta with grated cheese and chopped parsley. □

The next sauce is a bit of a problem in a minor sort of way, and there are versions of it which are overelaborate. This is because the writers of the recipes foolishly address themselves to the problem in the giving of the recipe instead of at the end, thus muddying the simplicity of the dish with a lot of high-church footwork that the cook would be better off inventing herself, or doing without.

CARBONARA

□ At each place setting put the following: some strips of crisp bacon that have been fried in a little olive oil, and a cup containing one well-beaten egg. In the center of the table put grated cheese and chopped parsley to pass.

Cook very thin spaghetti (vermicelli, or even capellini), drain it, put it into a hot deep serving dish, and bring it to the table along with enough hot deep bowls to serve everyone at the table.

Move fast. It's the heat of the pasta that's going to give the egg whatever cooking it gets, so don't hang around making small talk, or marking time while Aunt Gertrude goes to the bathroom. Dish up the pasta in the individual bowls and let the eaters pour on the egg, break up the bacon, and mix it all with parsley and cheese to their taste.   □

There. It's just bacon and eggs, Italian-style. If the thought of a raw egg turns your household off, you have my sympathy—but don't give up too easily. First of all, there is always plain butter, cheese, and parsley to offer them out of kindness; and of course peanut butter to push at them in pique. I would suggest, however, that you remind them that they already eat raw eggs without a single shudder in mayonnaise and egg nog. Urge them to repentance and better minds: It's their philosophy, not your cooking, that's giving them the creeps.

HAM SAUCE

□ Cut up ½ lb. good (that is, superb) ham into tiny dice. Any good country ham will do, but the uncooked cured hams do best: Prosciutto, Bauernschinken, Westphalian ham, etc. Fry the dice gently in ½ cup butter until crisp and golden.

Serve over pasta with etc.   □

ALL'AMATRICIANA OR ALLA MATRICANA

(You see this written both ways. I am not about to resolve the argument here, just to give you the recipe.)

□ Cut up ½ lb. slab bacon into dice, bruise a large clove of garlic, and fry the bacon and garlic in a little olive oil until the bacon is crisp and golden. At the end (or when the garlic gets too dark), throw out the garlic.

Add 1 cup Tomato Sauce (p. 107), season liberally with black pepper, and simmer for 5 minutes.

Serve over pasta.   □

There are fancier ways of making this, using only the fillets of peeled fresh tomatoes. In fact, there are Italian food buffs who order this dish in restaurants as a bellwether to find out if the chef really knows what he's doing. Still, it's good any way you make it, so enjoy it, even with the seeds.

SAUSAGE SAUCE

□ Prick ½ lb. Italian sausage (hot or sweet) with a skewer and parboil it in a little water for 5 minutes. Peel it immediately and chop it up a bit.

Chop up a small onion and simmer it in a few tablespoons of butter until it is soft and golden. Add the chopped sausage and simmer for 5 minutes.

Add 1 T. tomato paste, stir it in, and add a shy cup of dry white wine. Cook until the wine is almost gone and the sauce has a good consistency.

Check for salt and serve.   □

By the way, salt is best added rather earlier than late in the cooking process. The only thing you have to remember is that you must be discreet and make allowances for the eventual reduction of the sauce: water and wine will boil away nicely; but you're stuck with whatever salt you put in. Salt as you go for best results, therefore; but be careful.

CHICKEN-LIVER SAUCE

☐ Parboil a ¼-in. slice of salt pork for a few minutes, dice it up, and simmer it in a little butter until crisp and golden.

Cut up 8 or so chicken livers into decent-sized pieces and sauté them in the pan for a few minutes. (They should be barely cooked through.)

Add a shy cup of heavy cream, season with salt and pepper, and heat through without boiling.

Serve.

(Obviously, a little Marsala, or a touch of cognac . . .) ☐

GIBLET SAUCE

☐ Cook the gizzards and hearts from at least four chickens in 2 cups chicken stock until the stock is almost gone.

Chop them fine, peeling the gizzards first if you feel like it. Return them to the pot along with a large lump of butter, a splash of Marsala or Madeira, 1 T. tomato paste (or several tbs. Tomato Sauce, p. 107), and seasonings: a bay leaf, a pinch of thyme, rather a lot of pounded rosemary, a little grated lemon rind, a piece of stick cinnamon; add salt (careful!) and pepper, and simmer awhile until nicely blended.

Thin with additional stock if necessary, and serve.   ☐

There. Unless I have miscounted, that is an eight-gun salute from the meat side. Time now, however, for the real barrage.

Before we leave the Italian-style dishes, let me make good on a promise I made back in chapter three when I gave you the recipe for Spatchcocked Chicken with Red Sauce. You must learn how to steamroller a chicken. The British call this style of presentation Spatchock; the French, *à la crapaudine*. I settle simply for

FLATTENED CHICKEN (FOR ROASTING)

☐ Remove the backbone from a whole frying or broiling chicken. There are three ways to do this conveniently:

1. *With a Chinese cleaver:* pick up the chicken by the drumsticks with your left hand and hold it vertically so that the back of the bird faces you. Then, with short, light, chopping strokes of the cleaver make two cuts straight down, one on either side of the tail. The first few strokes are easy; but when you hit the hip joint you will have to be a little more aggressive. When you have gone through the hip in one of the cuts, do likewise in the other; then continue on down on both sides ad lib until you have taken out the back, neck and all.

2. *With a French chef's knife:* place the chicken on the cutting board, breast up, and insert a large, heavy chef's knife into the body cavity from the tail end. Position the knife on one side of the backbone, and push it straight through the chicken until the point comes out alongside the neck. Then, using both hands, bear down with all your weight and, with a rocking motion of the knife, cut straight through everything except the board. Repeat on the other side of the backbone.

3. *With poultry shears:* cut through the length of the bird on either side of the backbone.

In any case, when you have removed the backbone, spread the chicken, breast side up, on the board and, raising your glistening cleaver high in the golden sunlight, bring the flat of it down with a terrific *wham!* upon the tiny vertebrate. (Thank you, Monty Python.)

Tuck his wingtips under his shoulders, make two slits in the skin on either side of the hinder end of the breastbone and insert the ends of the drumsticks through them, arrange his legs in a presentable fashion so that they lie close upon the breast, brush him with oil, salt and pepper him, and roast him for an hour at 425°, basting occasionally.   □

There are a number of advantages to roasting a chicken in this fashion. First, since the legs cover parts of the breast, the breast cooks more slowly and is never overdone. Second, the bird is compact: you can roast it on one shelf and cook something else on another at the same time. Third, if you secure the bird in position with a couple of long metal skewers, it is in the best of all possible shapes for barbecuing.

But even if you don't cook it forthwith, a flattened chicken takes up far less room in the freezer than any other kind. Indeed, once flattened chickens are frozen hard, they can be stacked like books. If you are a bibliophile, you might even want to assign them acquisition numbers; but whatever you do, date and title everything you put in your freezer. That, of course, is a truism—the kind of thing that is usually taken as an insult by any intelligent person. In fact, however, truisms are simply truths which intelligent people need to have drummed into them more than other people do. The curse of the clever is their confidence that they will remember everything. But they don't, and that is that: ground beef, ground pork, and ground lamb all look alike after a month in the freezer, and as you know, they change places with each other faster than square dancers. A good cook, like a good lawyer, never bothers to remember anything he can simply look up when he needs it. Mark your freezer items, therefore, and save your mind for bigger things.

Like, for example, the following dishes made with the now easily located chopped meat of your choice.

HAMBURGERS *À LA* STEAK TARTARE

☐ To any kind of cheap ground beef, add minced onion, chopped capers, salt, and pepper, and mix well. Shape into patties and fry. (Make mine rare, please.) ☐

Any hamburger, by the way, profits by a little sauce. So, when the meat is done, put it on a warm plate and toss into the pan a couple of cubes of chicken stock and a splash of wine; add a lump of butter, swirl it all around to get the goodness out of the pan, reduce it to the consistency you like, and pour it over the meat.

How do you get chicken cubes? Aha! When you have gotten all the fat off your strained chicken stock, you simply freeze some of the stock in ice-cube trays. When it's hard, pop the cubes out of the trays into a plastic bag and store them in the freezer for any occasion when you need only a bit of stock at short notice. (Mark them, too: I have had guests who, when helping themselves to drinks, have ended up with Johnny Walker on the chicken rocks. No harm done, of course: builds you up as it tears you down, I always tell them. Still, it is a surprise.)

PARIS SNACKS

☐ Mix ½ lb. ground beef into the following: some soft breadcrumbs (from your trimmings in the freezer) soaked in milk; a little chopped caper, chopped gherkin, and chopped beet; and salt and white pepper to taste. (This dish is Swedish: hence the missing onion and black pepper.)

Work the mixture until it is well blended, and spread it thickly, crust to crust, on slices of bread.

Fry these on both sides in butter (meat side first) until a good color.

Serve—perhaps with fried eggs.   □

These can be made in advance and cooked as a lunch or late-night snack for company. They're rather pretty when they're done: the meat pulls in a bit from the edges of the bread and sits there like a little square hamburger gazing at you out of a toasty frame.

PEARL BALLS

□ Soak 1 cup Sticky Rice (also called Glutinous Rice, or Sweet Rice in Oriental groceries) in water overnight. Or do the same with ordinary short-grain rice.

Mix 1 lb. ground beef (or beef and pork) with the following: some minced onion and fresh ginger to taste; 1 T. cornstarch, 1 T. soy sauce, and 2 egg whites; and sherry, oil, salt, and pepper to taste.

Form the meat into balls, roll them in the drained rice so that they are completely covered, put them on an oiled plate, and steam for 20 minutes.

Serve as a first course or appetizer with condiments— white vinegar, hot mustard, soy sauce, coriander leaves, scallions, oyster sauce, etc.   □

STEAMED MEAT LOAF

□ Begin as above, but forget about the rice.

To the meat mixture add minced scallion, minced water chestnut, and minced black mushrooms (soaked first in boiling water) , all to taste.

Form the mixture into a single ball or loaf, put it on an oiled plate, and steam for 20 minutes.

Serve with condiments as above—and with rice, if it's your main course. □

We seem to have wandered into the Chinese repertory once again. Here are three more beef dishes. Get out the wok.

BEEF WITH PEPPER, ONION, AND TOMATOES

□ Mince 3 to 4 cloves garlic; rinse 2 to 3 T. Chinese salted black beans and mince; mince a slice of ginger; cut up 2 green peppers in 1-inch dice; dice 1 large onion to match; cut ½ lb. boneless raw lean beef into thin slices and marinate (see p. 11) ; cut two fresh tomatoes into wedges. Make a solution of cornstarch and cold water. Have at hand peanut oil, salt, 1 cup hot stock, dark soy sauce, and sugar.

Heat the wok very hot and add a little peanut oil and salt. Toss in the minced garlic and black bean, stir-fry for 30 seconds, add the green pepper and onion, stir-fry for another 30 seconds; add the stock, cover and boil for two minutes. Remove and set aside.

Heat the wok very hot again; add a little more oil and the minced ginger and stir-fry for 10 seconds; then add the sliced beef and stir-fry for 1 minute.

Return the pepper and onion mixture to the wok, bring to a boil, and add the following: 1 T. dark soy, a pinch of sugar, and cornstarch solution sufficient to thicken it nicely. Stir in the tomato wedges, heat through, check the seasoning, and serve. □

The beef for this dish is sliced in thin, squarish pieces to match the shapes of the other ingredients. For something different, here is a dish in which the beef is shredded—that is, cut into fine julienne to go with the matchsticks of celery made by cutting the stalks crosswise into two-inch pieces and then lengthwise into shreds.

SHREDDED BEEF AND CELERY

☐ Bruise 1 large clove garlic; shred 5 stalks celery (cut the stalks crosswise into 2-inch pieces, flatten the pieces with the side of the cleaver, and chop them lengthwise into fine julienne) ; shred ½ lb. boneless raw lean beef to match and marinate it (see p. 11). Make a thickening solution of cornstarch and cold water. Have at hand peanut oil, salt, and ½ cup hot stock.

Heat the wok very hot, add a little peanut oil and salt, and brown the garlic clove lightly; discard the garlic.

Add the celery to the wok, stir-fry briefly, add the stock, cover, and boil for two minutes; remove and set aside.

Heat the wok very hot again, add a little more oil, then the beef, and stir-fry for 1 minute.

Return the celery mixture to the wok, boil, thicken judiciously with the cornstarch mixture, check the seasoning, and serve.   ☐

But back to simple sliced beef for the last—with, of course, the broccoli stems sliced paper-thin crosswise for compatibility.

BEEF WITH BROCCOLI

☐ Mince a slice of fresh ginger; slice up 1 lb. or so of broccoli, leaving the flowerets in larger pieces; slice thin ½ lb. boneless raw lean beef; make a thickening solution of cornstarch and cold water; have at hand peanut oil, salt, dark soy, and 1 cup hot stock.

Heat the wok very hot, add a little peanut oil and salt, add the ginger, and stir-fry for 10 seconds; add the broccoli and stir-fry for 30 seconds; then add the stock, cover, and boil for 3 to 5 minutes, or until barely tender; remove and set aside.

Heat the wok very hot again, add a little more oil; then add the beef, stir-fry for 1 minute, and add 1 T. dark soy.

Return the broccoli mixture to the wok, boil, thicken judiciously with the cornstarch mixture, check the seasoning, and serve.   □

But just to prove that I am not unreasonably prejudiced against steaks, let me give you a recipe which stretches a single steak into a meal for six or eight and wakes up their taste buds in the bargain.

STEAK AND SALAD, THAI-STYLE

□ In a large bowl or pot, assemble the salad ingredients: 1 head romaine, broken up; 1 red onion, sliced; 1 cucumber, peeled and sliced; 2 scallions, cut into 1-in. pieces; a dozen or so fresh mint leaves; a like amount of fresh basil; and twice as many fresh coriander (Chinese parsley) leaves. Chill till needed.

Make the dressing: Oriental Fish Sauce and fresh lime juice (in the proportion three parts to two), seasoned with minced garlic and fresh ginger, and crushed hot red pepper. (Two notes: 1. The fish sauce is available in Oriental groceries; soy sauce is a possible substitute, but it's not the same at all. 2. If you can get Thai pepper, do so; it is without doubt the hottest, most fragrant stuff on earth. In any case though, be judicious when you make the dressing: the dish is supposed to be very hot, but if your guests are not used to fiery tastes, go light and let the stronger souls add more red pepper at the table.)

When you're ready, simply grill a steak over charcoal, keeping it rare; then slice it thin, add it to the salad, pour on the dressing, toss well, and serve—with extra condiments if you like, and perhaps some crushed roasted peanuts to sprinkle around.   □

XII

IN SOLITUDE, FOR COMPANY

It occurs to me, however, that I have not given you directions for making brown stock. Let me rectify that omission before moving on.

The differences between brown and white stock are essentially two: the scraps of bone, fat, and meat (beef or veal) are browned for a good while in the oven before they are added to the stock pot; and the seasonings are (at least for my taste) a little different. About the meat: obviously, the more you use, the richer your stock will be. Given a respectable quantity of beef and some extra marrow bones, it will become a reasonably hearty soup in its own right; given more meat and a knuckle of veal, it will be well on its way to becoming consommé. But then any cookbook can teach you that. I want you to learn how to make plain brown stock out of nothing but the leavings of the chuck steaks you bone out at home.

BROWN STOCK

☐ As you bone out chuck steaks, freeze all the pieces of bone, fat, and scrap in a plastic bag.

When you have accumulated the remains of four or more, put them in a roasting pan (it's unnecessary to thaw them), add a little water to the pan, and put it into a 375°

oven. Move them about till they separate, and baste occasionally.

When they have had an hour, or are beginning to take on a good color, add a couple of sliced onions and sliced carrots to the pan and continue browning, being careful that the vegetables become only a flavorsome brown, not a bitter black.

An interruption is in order. The color of brown stock comes from the caramelization of the natural sugar in the ingredients. Beef has a fair amount all by itself, but onions and carrots have still more: hence the time spent in browning. Once you understand the principle, however, you will realize that even completely finished white stock can be browned, if you have the patience: you put a small amount of it in a flat pan and, either in the oven or on top of the stove you boil it away and let the residue brown. Then you add some more stock, stirring well to loosen the already browned deposit, and boil it away and let it brown again. Just repeat the process until you reach a color that will be satisfactory when the remainder of the stock is finally added; then put it all in and stir it up thoroughly for the last time. Obviously, what you now have is not only browned, but concentrated as well. It should be delicious all by itself. It will definitely make splendid sauces.

In any case, the crucial thing is to get all the color out of the browning pan into the stock. Hence the next step.

Put the browned scraps and vegetables into a stockpot and, setting the roasting pan on top of the stove, add hot water to it, turn up the heat, and stir and scrape the pan to color the water. Empty the water into the stockpot, and repeat until the pan is clean.

To the stockpot now add chopped vegetables to taste: some more onion and carrot if you like, and certainly celery and parsley. Add herbs and spices: a little thyme, a bay leaf, a clove, some marjoram, a blade or two of mace, a sprinkling of whole black peppercorns, and very little salt.

Cover with more water to the depth of your thumb, bring to a boil, skim off the untidy froth that rises to the top, and simmer for several hours.

Strain, cool quickly, and refrigerate. When it's cold, cut the cake of fat off the top and freeze the stock in containers or ice cube trays as desired.

If, when you use the stock, you want something richer, simply boil it down by half or more to the desired strength. □

About the fat: put it in a deepish saucepan with some water, boil it for five minutes or so, run it all through a clean coffee filter, and refrigerate. When it's thoroughly cold again, remove the cake of fat from the water (if the water is jellied, save it: it's stock again), scrape away any fine particles from the underside, dry it off, wrap it up, and freeze or refrigerate it until you need fat for deep frying. If you make stock even ten times a year, this should keep you supplied perpetually. It makes particularly tasty French fries; and if you boil it up with water and filter it again from time to time, it will refresh itself nicely. If it's not too far gone, it can even be added to the next batch of fat you make from the succeeding pot of stock.

While we're on the subject of scraps though, let me give you two recipes for pork sausage to keep in the back of your mind when you bone out pork shoulders. The amounts given are for a pound of meat: govern yourself accordingly.

BREAKFAST SAUSAGE

□ Take a pound of boneless raw pork chunks. (I like my sausage with a fair amount of fat in it: 4/5 lean to 1/5 fat; you will do as you like, but lean pork only makes a rather dry product.) Put the chunks in a bowl and add 1 tsp. salt, a generous ½ tsp. each of ground black pepper and sage, and a good pinch of red pepper. Mix well, and let it sit awhile if you like.

Then chop it up to your liking: twice through the coarse blade of a grinder does nicely; so does a comparable effort with a Chinese cleaver.

Shape it into a fat roll, or rolls; wrap and freeze.   □

Some notes: first, there is nothing to stop you from frying up a bit of it before wrapping: it provides you with a rewarding snack, and it allows you to make any corrections in the seasoning of the mixture that your taste calls for. Second, I have not bothered to say anything about stuffing the sausage meat into casings because that's more work —for less result—than you need: well-browned sausage patties are every bit as acceptable as links. Finally, a word about pinches: if you want a tiny pinch of some dry ingredient, put your thumb and forefingers, already joined, into the substance and pick up what you can simply by flexing them a bit; if you want a generous pinch, put them in separated and take out all you can get by joining them. If you have fat fingers, make allowances; but remember, that may be God's way of telling you to eat well-spiced food.

CHORIZO

□ Put 1 lb. boneless raw pork chunks (4/5 lean, 1/5 fat) into a bowl and add the following: 2 T. vinegar; 2 T. water; 1 clove garlic, crushed; a generous pinch each of black pepper, red pepper, and cumin; 1 T. paprika; 1 tsp. oregano; and 1 tsp. salt.

Mix well, let it marinate awhile, and chop or grind it to your liking (not too fine though, if you please).

Fry up a sample, adjust the seasonings if necessary, wrap, and refrigerate or freeze.   □

While we're in this neighborhood, here's something worth remembering, especially since most people's supply of chili powder is usually rather far over the hill.

CHILI POWDER

☐ Combine 1 part each of salt, garlic powder, and cumin and 3 parts each of red pepper, oregano, and paprika. Pound them in a mortar, or pulverize them in a blender (if you're still in a cheating mood), until fine.   ☐

The characteristic taste of chili powder, as you will see, is not—except for its fieriness—chili pepper. It is cumin and oregano. Sometimes black pepper is added as well, but I usually leave it out. If you put it in, decide the proportion yourself. The main thing I am concerned with here is to give you a way of making chili powder fresh when you need it: when all the ingredients are pulverized, there is a fragrance you get no other way.

Which leads me, naturally, to the recipe for the world's simplest and best chili. I have no intention of involving myself in the great and interminable debate that goes on in this country about the subject: I know you think you know a better version. But if you will promise not to send it to me, I shall promise to be brief.

CHILI

☐ Put some bite-size chunks of beef in a bowl and mix them with a lot of chili powder.

Heat some lard or oil in a pot, put in the meat, stir it around, and add a can of beef bouillon.

Cook till the meat is very tender and the sauce is well reduced and flavorful. Serve with rice and beans.   ☐

How big is a bite-size chunk? Dear me. When I teach theology, I remind my students frequently that most of the mischief in the subject comes not from the answers it gives (those, after all, are the work of theologians and therefore invariably clever, at least) ; it comes, rather, from the questions asked—and, of course, from the foolishness of answering them at all. For example, suppose you were to ask me why, if God is good, the world is bad. I could spend (in fact, I have spent) an entire book trying to distinguish and subdistinguish my way out of the bind you put me in. In fact, however, your question—like all important ones—is not so much an inquiry as it is part of a lover's quarrel into which I would be ill-advised to butt. The only proper answer for me to give you is itself a question: Why, if your wife loves you, does she spend so much energy giving you a hard time? To which you would no doubt reply that God is supposed to be better than your wife. But that in turn (setting aside the fact that Scripture provides only shaky support for such an assumption), gives me my next rejoinder: Why then do you spend more time on your wife than you do on God? To which the answer has to be that you love your wife rather more diligently than you love God. But that's all right. It's not a shame, it's an opening: when, as, and if you get something proportionate going with God, you will find the nerve to put up with his bad manners too. So ends every honest theological dialogue—and every straightforward culinary one as well.

A bite-size chunk is as big as a bite. How big is that? Well, the foolish answer is any answer that takes the question at face value. For example, the average American male, when screaming the word "Help!" can part his teeth to the extent of something like $1\frac{1}{2}$ to $1\frac{3}{4}$ inches. As that is not seemly at the dinner table, however, we shall have to fix bite-size at rather less. Accordingly, some other vocable, uttered with less urgency but more enthusiasm, must be found as a criterion. I suggest the second syllable of the word "incredible," as in the phrase "incredibly delicious." Now, if you will simply fetch a ruler, go to the mirror, pronounce the words, and measure the gap between your upper and lower incisors at the very moment of the short *e* . . .

But you see. If you loved chili enough to cry out for it, desire would lead you to put up with any size bite that gave you chili at all—or, alternatively, to live with the strictest and most limited definition of it in the world. The lover's answer, even when it's silly, is always the right answer: it settles not the question but the questioner, which was the real point all along. Settle yourself, therefore: make a pot of chili. Oh, taste and see . . .

As long as we are on bits and pieces, I think I shall introduce you to one more style of cooking in the Chinese repertory. We have already done *chow,* or stir-fried, dishes, and *jing,* or steamed, dishes; here are a few recipes using the method called Red cooking. Essentially, they involve the boiling of meats in a mixture of soy sauce, water, and seasonings. First then,

RED-COOKED CHICKEN WINGS

☐ Make the red-cooking sauce: into a pot large enough to hold your collection of chicken wings, put the following: 1 cup light soy sauce, 1 cup dark soy sauce (or 2 cups good Japanese soy sauce), and a generous cup of water; add a thick slice of fresh ginger, lightly smashed; a clove of garlic, bruised; 4 T. sugar; 1 star anise (from a Chinese grocery—anise extract or a little anisette will do as a substitute); and 2 T. sherry.

Simmer the wings in this sauce for 20 minutes, or until done to your liking.

Serve hot or cold. ☐

Strain the sauce into a container, and refrigerate or freeze it for reuse with other red-cooked dishes, such as:

RED-COOKED CHICKEN LIVERS

□ Trim some whole chicken livers and poach them in red-cooking sauce until they are just done.

Cool, slice, and serve as an appetizer, with a little of the sauce sprinkled on top.   □

RED-COOKED EGGS

□ Cook up some eggs as follows: bring a pot of water to a boil and gently put into it 6 eggs from the refrigerator. When the water returns to a boil, give them exactly 5 minutes. Then take the pot to the sink and run cold water over the eggs for 5 minutes. (This leaves the centers of the yolks slightly underdone.)

Peel the eggs carefully and soak them overnight in a jar of leftover red-cooking sauce. (This makes the outsides of the whites a pleasing, flavorful brown.)

Slice in quarters lengthwise and serve as an appetizer with a little of the sauce for dipping—or use them as a garnish for other dishes.   □

Obviously, this method (with a larger amount of the same sauce) can be used for poaching a whole chicken—or, to use less sauce, for poaching a flattened chicken (p. 174). Other whole cuts of meat can be cooked in the same way with slight variations.

RED-COOKED LAMB

□ Take a small leg of lamb and simmer it until done (2 hours or so) in red-cooking sauce to which some scallions cut into short lengths have been added.

Serve hot or cold.   □

RED-COOKED BEEF (CHINESE POT ROAST)

☐ Tie a piece of beef for pot roasting and sear it on all sides in a little oil in a Dutch oven or wok.

Adjust the basic recipe for red-cooking sauce by adding some more sugar and changing the proportion of water to soy sauce—instead of 1 part water to 2 parts soy, use 3 parts water to 2 parts soy.

Simmer the beef in the sauce until done. (Vegetables can be added at the appropriate time if you like: turnip, carrot, etc. Just don't let them get too soft.)

Serve hot in slices, with the vegetables and some sauce, over rice. Or serve cold for a buffet.   ☐

As I said earlier, this is elegant when nicely presented: slice the pot roast cold and arrange it tastefully on a large platter, sprinkling some sauce on the pieces as you go. Surround the whole with a border of quartered fresh tomatoes, quartered Red-cooked Eggs (p. 190), and scallion flowers.

Scallion flowers? Simple. Trim some whole scallions until they are fresh-looking and, starting from the bulb end, cut two 1½-inch pieces off of each. Then, with a knife, cut through the upper ¾ inch of each piece three or four times lengthwise, rolling the piece a little for each cut so that the knife goes right through the diameter of the scallion. Put them in a bowl of cold water and refrigerate. They will open into flowers all by themselves. (Don't throw away the green tops: chop some of them for sprinkling over the finished platter, and freeze the rest with your vegetable scraps for stock.)

We seem to have arrived without warning at the Chinese cold buffet, and it occurs to me I have said next to nothing in this book about entertaining and its relationship to your renewal. That is, of course, quite natural: resurrection, except for the all-important company of the one who raises you, is a rather intimate and personal business. We have necessarily been a bit preoccupied with our insides and our immediate surroundings. But as Auden said, we live "in solitude, for company," and if Lazarus or Old Dead Ernest doesn't throw a little dinner party sooner or later, it can only mean he has missed the point of what has been done to him. The main invitation in life is to the Supper of the Lamb in Jerusalem, if not this year or next, at least forever—which should be good enough for anyone.

Accordingly, if you are genuinely alive at all, you will entertain; and I urge you to do it as early in the game as possible. If you are in groups one or three, you will probably be ready for it quite on your own. But if you are in group two, that is, widowed, divorced, separated, ostracized, or in any other way more aware of lostness of life than most, I want to give you a push—no, it must be stronger— a shove, a firm, swift kick in the direction of dinnering. For you need company in direct proportion to the degree you feel yourself unfit for it.

The reasons for that feeling are as negligible as they are predictable. Whether you feel lonely because you have lost the company that made all company bright, or unfit because the garbage of guilt is so regularly, if uninvitedly, delivered to your door, or even reprehensible because you are still going out every day and bringing home the grapefruit rinds and fish skeletons of your past—the hole you are in is not a home, and you will never be able to make it such until you fill it frequently with friends. Even the companionship of the one who raised you is not enough to do the trick. Jesus and Lazarus didn't go off to toast marshmallows by themselves: At the beginning of chapter twelve of the Gospel, right after Lazarus's spectacular comeback in chapter eleven, John shows us the two of them sitting down to one of Martha's Sabbath suppers to fold a little gefilte fish and chicken soup into the system before the rigors of Palm Sunday.

Not everyone will necessarily be pleased with your public performances: it was after that particular supper that the chief priests got the bright idea that Lazarus had to go too. It's just that there is no way of being raised that doesn't involve acting risen. Hence your Thursday evenings *chez soi* or *chez nous,* your dress-up Saturday dinners for six or eight, and your alfresco Sunday night suppers for as many as will park their twelve-cylinder guiltspreaders elsewhere. Blame only tells you what you already knew—that you are dead. The company of the forgiving and the forgiven is what you need if you are to celebrate the life—in and with that death—you have been given. With that preface, therefore, the Chinese Buffet.

Let me list a suitable selection of dishes and then catch you up with the necessary recipes.

CHINESE BUFFET

Red-cooked Beef
Cold Lo Mein
Barbecued Spare Ribs
Puff Shrimp or Shrimp Toast
Hacked Chicken
Chicken Skin and Cucumber Salad
Red-cooked Chicken Wings and Chicken Livers

I would be conning you if I didn't say that this is a bit of work. But if you don't mind spending a Saturday puttering in the kitchen, most of the heavy labor will be behind you when you come to putting in the hour or so on Sunday afternoon that you'll need to lay it out. Besides, it's not all that expensive: if you've been boning out chickens and pork shoulders as you go, the only new things you'll have to buy are a 5-pound piece of beef for pot roasting, two boxes of spaghettini or fine linguine, a rack of spare ribs, and a pound or so of shrimp.

About quantities, just remember that the Chinese menu operates on the principle of variety, not quantity. If you're serving eight, for example, you don't make one huge batch of a single dish; you make two-person servings of four or five different dishes and let the guests sample their way through the supper. My suggested menu contains seven dishes; accordingly, it should do nicely for fourteen or more, especially since the Red-cooked Beef and the Cold Lo Mein are ample presentations and will provide liberal seconds for guests with hollow legs. On with it then, in the order listed. Just remember that any one of the dishes is good all by itself—even when you're all by yourself.

Red-cooked Beef: Cook up your 5-pound pot roast (p. 191), slice it into at least thirty pieces, and arrange it with tomatoes, Red-cooked Eggs, and scallion flowers.

Cold Lo Mein: I must back up a bit and teach you how to make Chinese Roast Pork so you always have a supply in the freezer.

CHINESE ROAST PORK

☐ Into a saucepan put: 1 tsp. brown bean sauce (buy a can from a Chinese grocery; the remainder can be kept in a covered jar in the refrigerator indefinitely) ; 1 clove garlic, crushed; ½ cup stock or water; 2 T. salt; 4 T. sugar; 1 T. soy sauce; ½ tsp. five spice powder (Chinese again: it keeps indefinitely—anisette plus black pepper, clove, and cinnamon will come close as a substitute) ; 1 tsp. tomato paste; and 1 tsp. sherry. Heat to blend.

Marinate four ½-lb. pieces of lean boned raw pork (nice, compact little billets, if possible) for 6 hours or so in the mixture.

When you're ready to cook the pork, put a drip pan

with some water in it on the bottom of the oven and heat
the oven to 450°. Take the pieces of pork out of the marinade and put them directly onto a rack over the drip pan.
Give them 15 minutes at 450°, and another 15 minutes or
so at 350°.

Cool, wrap, and refrigerate or freeze.   ☐

Now we're ready for

COLD LO MEIN (CHINESE COLD NOODLE SALAD)

☐ Cook 2 lbs. spaghettini or fine linguine (or fresh Chinese
noodles if you can get them or make them) until they are
al dente. Don't make mush. Drain, and run cold water
through them until they are cool.

Put them into a bowl and add the following: peanut
oil and sesame oil (in the proportion 2 to 1) to coat
them nicely; Chinese Roast Pork (above), sliced and then
shredded into fine julienne (use a ½-lb. piece of roast pork
for each 1-lb. box of pasta) ; ½ lb. bean sprouts cooked
briefly in the wok with a little ginger and soy sauce (or
a comparable quantity of julienne of celery and carrot
dropped for a minute into boiling water) ; a generous
amount of chopped scallion; and pepper, sugar, oyster
sauce (or soy) , and salt, all to taste.

Mix well, cover, and store in the refrigerator till
needed. Then, correct the seasoning, dish up, and serve.   ☐

Barbecued Spare Ribs are the next item on the agenda.
At long last you get a chance to be really heavy-handed with
a cleaver.

BARBECUED SPARE RIBS

☐ Cut a rack of spare ribs apart with a cleaver. Then chop the longer ribs in pieces crosswise so that all your pieces are something like 4 in. in length.

Make a marinade: into a saucepan put 1 tsp. brown bean sauce; 4 cloves garlic, crushed; ½ cup water; 4 T. hoisin sauce (Chinese grocery, once more: store it like brown bean sauce); 4 T. sugar; 4 T. dark soy sauce; and 1 T. sherry. Heat a bit to blend, pour over the cut-up ribs, and marinate 6 hours or more.

Put the ribs, with the marinade, in one layer in a shallow pan and bake at 350° for an hour or so, turning occasionally. They should be a good color, but not blackened and dry.   ☐

You note, of course, that these are not actually barbecued. That's because they're going on a buffet. If you want to barbecue them, just cut the oven time down a bit, chill the ribs in the sauce till you need them, and then let your guests put a good color on them over the hibachi in the yard.

Puff Shrimp or *Shrimp Toast* belong under seafood. The order of this chapter is already so tenuous that I am concerned for what little is left. Sorry; turn to p. 220 or p. 97.

Hacked Chicken and *Chicken Skin and Cucumber Salad* go together, coming, as they do, from a single bird.

HACKED CHICKEN

☐ Cut off the wings of a whole chicken or a flattened chicken (p. 174), and reserve. Poach the bird in stock to cover, to which a piece of smashed ginger has been added. Give it 12 minutes on each side, and then let it cool in the stock. Strain and save the stock.

Skin the chicken, keeping the pieces of skin as large as possible. Cover the skin and reserve it.

Bone out all the meat, once again keeping the pieces as large as possible.

Hack the breast meat into good-size julienne. Put it in a bowl, add a very little peanut oil, light soy, and finely shredded ginger; cover and chill.

Cut up the dark meat likewise. Put it in a bowl and mix it with a sauce of the following: hot sesame oil, crushed garlic, hoisin sauce, light soy, and vinegar, all to taste—heated a bit to blend the ingredients. Chill. (This dish should be very, very aggressive. If you go light on the hot oil when you make it, at least put the bottle on the buffet next to the dish so the fire-eaters can be happy.)

Serve the two kinds of chicken at opposite ends of the same bowl, garnish with coriander leaves and/or chopped scallion, and let the guests decide for themselves.   □

Chicken Skin and Cucumber Salad is one of those dishes which, when you tell people about it, is first taken as some kind of joke, but then, once they see you're serious, viewed with unadulterated alarm. In fact, however, it is very good and, in its own violently mustardy way, quite refreshing. Just warn your guests that, like all such preparations, it is capable of socking them right at the base of the skull.

CHICKEN SKIN AND CUCUMBER SALAD

□ Cover a large handful of wood ear mushrooms (also called tree ears or cloud's ears, these are sold dried by Oriental groceries and keep indefinitely in a covered jar) with boiling water and let them soak for 15 minutes. Pick out the tough centers if you're being careful.

Cut a large cucumber (peeled only if you like—or if it's one of those waxed jobbies) in half lengthwise, scrape out the seeds with the point of a teaspoon, slice it thin crosswise, and salt it lightly.

Cut the reserved chicken skin into bite-size pieces.

Put the sliced cucumber in a shallow serving bowl, garnish nicely with the wood ears and chicken skin, and chill.

Make the sauce: in a bowl combine 1 T. light soy sauce, 2 tsp. sesame oil, 1 T. sherry, 1 T. vinegar, 4 tsp. dry mustard, 1 tsp. sugar, and salt to taste. Mix and let stand for 15 minutes.

When you set the dish out, simply pour the sauce over the ingredients in the serving bowl and let the guests mix it up as they help themselves.   □

Red-cooked Chicken Wings and Livers are on p. 189–90. Just dish them up attractively and sprinkle with chopped scallion. (By the way, chop the whole scallion, green part and all. There are not only two colors to this versatile vegetable, but two flavors as well. Americans all too often miss out on the green taste.)

Perhaps the best way to end this chapter is to give you a straightforward compendium of Chinese recipes and let you pore over them at your leisure. Before I do, though, I want to give you a pair of hot and spicy advices that the last two fiery concoctions have brought to mind: the general procedure for making a Chinese curry; and a sockdolager of a noodle dish called Sam Jup Mein, or Three-flavor Noodles.

CHINESE CURRY

□ Using ½ lb. raw boned meat—chicken, beef, pork, or lamb—or ½ lb. peeled raw shrimp, cut up the meat into uniform slices or julienne, as you like. Small shrimp may be left whole.

Cut a good-size onion in half lengthwise and then slice it up crosswise (or cut it to match your meat).

Put a very low fire under a dry wok, add to it 4 T. curry powder (yes, *four*) along with the cut-up onion, and stir it around for a couple of minutes until the whole house is pungent.

Then add the meat, stir everything for another couple of minutes, put in ½ cup stock or water, and turn the fire up high.

Add salt, sugar, and black pepper to taste and cook until the meat, or whatever, is done. (Beef and shrimp should be barely cooked; use your judgment about chicken or pork.)

At the end, thicken discreetly with cornstarch solution and serve over plain rice.   □

SAM JUP MEIN (THREE-FLAVOR NOODLES)

□ Cook ½ lb. fresh Chinese noodles (or ½ lb. spaghettini) *al dente.*

Meanwhile, slice half a large onion in thin half-rings; cut a little Chinese Roast Pork (p. 194) into fine julienne; cut a large fresh tomato into wedges; and mix together ½ cup tomato catsup, 1 tsp. hoisin sauce, and salt, sugar, and black pepper to taste.

Put a very low flame under a dry wok and add to it 3 T. curry powder and the sliced onion. Stir for a couple of minutes.

Add the roast pork and ⅓ cup stock or water, and turn the fire up high. Bring to a boil, add the catsup mixture, stir and boil again, and at the last minute add the cut-up tomato.

Drain the pasta, put it in a bowl, pour the sauce over all, and serve.   □

Now, however, for the armamentarium of chicken and pork recipes, beginning with two steamer-launched dishes and ending with a bandolier of simple stir-fried delights.

STEAMED SPARE RIBS WITH BLACK BEAN

☐ Separate 1 lb. spare ribs and chop them into 1-in. pieces with a cleaver. Drop them into boiling water and parboil for 5 minutes. Drain, and reserve the water.

Rinse 3 T. Chinese black beans and chop them a bit. Mince 5 cloves garlic, chop up a scallion into ½-in. pieces, put them all in a bowl, and add the following: 1 tsp. salt, 1 T. peanut oil, 1 T. sherry, 3 T. sugar, ½ tsp. cornstarch, 2 T. vinegar and 2 T. of the water you boiled the pork in. Add the pieces of ribs, mix well, and empty the contents of the bowl onto a serving dish that will fit the wok (or the steamer) you're going to use.

Steam 45 minutes, or until tender, and serve with plain rice.   ☐

STEAMED CHICKEN

☐ Soak 5 or 6 dried black Chinese mushrooms in boiling water for 15 minutes.

Chop half a raw chicken, bones and all, into bite-size pieces, and mix it into a marinade made of: 2 tsp. peanut oil, 1 tsp. dark soy sauce, 1 tsp. sherry, ½ tsp. sugar, ½ tsp. cornstarch, a dash of black pepper, and salt to taste.

Shred the mushrooms into fine julienne, shred 4 paper-thin slices fresh ginger very fine, and slice ¼ cup each bamboo shoots and water chestnuts. Add all to the marinating chicken.

Put everything in a suitable serving dish (the flatter, the better), and steam 7 to 10 minutes, or until done. Serve with plain rice.   ☐

I just realized I have not told you the Chinese way of mincing garlic. You must learn it; it's the greatest labor-saver in the world. Put the unpeeled clove of garlic on the cutting board and, with the flat of the cleaver, give it a light but firm tap. That loosens the skin: peel it off with your fingers. Put the clove back on the board and, bringing the flat of the cleaver down squarely, smash it to a pulp with one decisive smack. That's it. Think of all those wasted years. And remember, you mince a slice of fresh ginger the same way.

PORK AND OYSTER SAUCE

☐ Mince a slice of fresh ginger. Cut ½ lb. boneless raw lean pork into thin slices and marinate (see p. 11). Have at hand peanut oil, salt, ½ cup hot stock, black pepper, oyster sauce, and a thickening solution of cornstarch mixed with cold water.

Heat the wok very hot, add a little peanut oil and salt, then add the ginger and stir-fry 10 seconds; add the pork and stir-fry 3 minutes; add the stock and boil for 1 minute. Season with black pepper and 2 T. oyster sauce, thicken with the cornstarch mixture, check the seasoning, and serve.   ☐

The next dish uses pickled mustard cabbage, which is available only in Chinese groceries. Fresh (not canned) sauerkraut makes a decent substitute, though it lacks the pungency of the original. Still, the dish is refreshing either way, so be sure to try it.

PORK AND PICKLED MUSTARD CABBAGE
(OR SAUERKRAUT)

☐ Cut up mustard cabbage into bite-size pieces; cut ½ lb. boneless raw lean pork into thin slices and marinate (see

p. 11). Have at hand peanut oil, sugar, vinegar, ½ cup hot stock, and a thickening solution of cornstarch mixed with cold water.

Heat the wok moderately, add a little peanut oil, then add the pickled cabbage and some sugar and vinegar to taste (start with 2 T. sugar and 1 tsp. vinegar and go from there) ; stir-fry for 3 minutes, remove, and set aside.

Heat the wok very hot, add a little more oil, then the pork, and stir-fry for 3 minutes.

Add the stock, return the cabbage to the wok, boil, thicken with the cornstarch mixture, check the seasoning, and serve.   □

The next dish, a recent rage in Chinese restaurants, can be made at home. Maybe later I'll tell you how to make the pancakes—the Chinese doilies, or *bing*—in which it's usually wrapped. For now though, just the recipe for the filling, which is good all by itself. Lily flowers, by the way, are another dry Chinese ingredient from the Oriental grocery. If you can't get them, make the dish anyway.

MOO SHEE PORK

□ Break 4 eggs into a bowl, season, and beat lightly. Mince a slice of fresh ginger; shred 2 oz. boneless raw lean pork; shred ½ cup head cabbage; soak 10 wood ears and 6 lily flowers in hot water for 15 minutes; shred 1 or 2 scallions (cut them into 2-inch lengths, flatten the pieces a bit with the side of the cleaver, and chop them lengthwise into fine julienne) ; have at hand peanut oil, salt, sherry, light soy sauce, sugar, and black pepper.

Heat the wok hot, add a little peanut oil, scramble the eggs, remove, and set aside.

Again, heat the wok very hot, add a little oil and salt, then the ginger, and stir-fry for 10 seconds; add the pork and stir-fry for 30 seconds; add a generous splash of sherry, then the cabbage, the wood ears, and the lily flowers, and stir-fry for 1 minute; add 2 tsp. light soy sauce, a pinch of sugar, a turn of black pepper, and the scallion. Return the eggs to the wok, mix well, heat through, and serve.   □

Of course, if you want to have the effect of the pancake wrappers without waiting for me to get around to the recipe, you can always fry the eggs into eight very thin, nicely brown omelets. Just use a small frying pan and a fair amount of peanut oil, put in an eighth of the beaten egg mixture at a time, swirl it around to coat the bottom of the pan, let the first side brown nicely, then turn your egg doily over carefully and give it a few seconds on the other side. Put them on an oiled plate and keep them warm while you whip up the rest of the dish.

CHICKEN WITH BROWN BEAN SAUCE

□ Cut some boneless raw chicken (two breasts, or the equivalent) into ¾-inch dice and marinate (see p. 11), but add sufficient cornstarch to the mixture to coat the pieces of chicken with a batter the consistency of very heavy cream or thin paste. Mince a clove of garlic and a slice of fresh ginger; soak 8 Chinese dried black mushrooms in hot water for 15 minutes and dice; dice ⅓ cup bamboo shoots and 1 green pepper. Have at hand 2 cups peanut oil, ½ cup hot stock, brown bean sauce, hot sesame oil, and a thickening solution of cornstarch mixed with cold water.

Heat 2 cups peanut oil in the wok to frying temperature (test by putting a wooden chopstick into the oil from time to time as it heats up: when bubbles come out of the wood fairly promptly, the oil is hot enough). Deep-fry the chicken pieces to a nice color; remove and set aside; pour the oil out of the wok.

Heat the wok hot, add the garlic and ginger, and stir-fry 10 seconds; add the mushrooms, the bamboo shoots, and the green pepper, and stir-fry for 30 seconds. Add the stock, cover, and boil for 1 minute.

Return the chicken to the wok, add 2 T. brown bean sauce, boil, thicken with the cornstarch mixture, check the seasoning, add 1 T. (more or less) hot sesame oil, mix well, and serve.   □

DICED CHICKEN WITH ALMONDS

□ Mince 1 slice fresh ginger. Dice the following: 1 cup Chinese cabbage, ½ cup fresh mushrooms, 4 water chestnuts, ¼ cup celery, ½ cup bamboo shoots, 12 snow peas, and 2 chicken breasts. Have at hand peanut oil, salt, ½ cup hot stock, a thickening solution of cornstarch mixed with cold water, and a generous handful of toasted almonds.

Heat the wok hot, add a little peanut oil and salt, then add the ginger, and stir-fry 10 seconds; add the Chinese cabbage, the mushrooms, the water chestnuts, the celery and the bamboo shoots, and stir-fry 30 seconds; add the stock, cover, and boil for 2 minutes. Remove all and set aside.

Heat the wok very hot, add a little more oil and salt, then the chicken, and stir-fry 1 minute.

Return the first mixture to the wok, boil, add the snow peas, thicken with the cornstarch mixture, check the seasoning, and dish up.

Sprinkle the dish with toasted almonds, and serve.   □

To make toasted almonds, put a ¼-inch layer of salt in the bottom of a small, heavy frying pan, add whole blanched almonds, and brown them nicely over a medium flame, stirring *constantly*—they burn the minute you turn your back. Garnish the finished presentation with the almonds and save the salt for Chinese cooking.

Chinese cabbage, or *bok choy*, may not be available. Substitute the thicker parts of ordinary cabbage and cook it a little longer.

There. My debt has been discharged with style: I have yet to meet anybody who doesn't like this one.

XIII

THE OLDEST FIELD

S o much for meat. Actually, it is really so little; but that's inevitable. This book is about your renewal as a cook; all it aims to do is pique, or repique, your interest in yourself as you stand at the stove. Please note that. It is a project for which no mere pile of recipes, however numerous or commendable they may be, is adequate. What is needed is not a mass of novel and detailed instructions, but the smallest handful of new principles—not a vast array of life-support machinery to keep you going in the midst of the death, culinary or otherwise, in which you find yourself, but a radically new life which, in and with that death, will surprise you, as life always does, by taking care of itself.

I have, accordingly, urged upon you only the necessary little, not the gratuitous much: a simplification of seasonings, an economy of equipment, a variety of vegetables, an aggrandizement of grains, and a break with beef. There remains, however, one more field where a simple change of attitude, coupled with a few recipes involving basic principles, will produce a startling result. That field is the granddaddy of them all: the sea.

But where is seafood in the American diet? Unfortunately, out to lunch: Save for tuna sandwiches, it is not a significant part of most people's cookery. Oh, from time to time you may find an occasional tuna–potato chip casserole (made, invariably, with canned mushroom soup) on the supper table—and some kind of Newburg held in reserve for gourmet dinners—but most cooks simply don't know what to do with fish. That is partly because good fresh fish is not as available as it should be; but it is mostly because the whole subject has been allowed to slip into virtual oblivion. We eat fish only when we're either desperate or putting on the dog: nothing can be given that combination of cold shoulder and hot hands and remain an object of love very long. If you spoke to your husband only when you needed either a hand with the garbage or an escort in a tux, you would soon enough find yourself—and him—looking elsewhere for a lover. It is the vast middle ground of ordinary contact where we need to meet our fellow creatures in delight; and nowhere is that truer than in cookery.

I have always cringed at the use of the word "gourmet" to describe dishes. It is first snobbish, second silly, and finally a disservice to food. Snobbish because it implies that there are only an initiated few with tastes sufficiently refined to appreciate the confections in question. Silly because it imports into the subject of cookery totally alien criteria: To ask if Red Anchovy Sauce is a gourmet dish—or to decide that it isn't—is as foolish as amassing your collection of records on the basis of their suitability as background music for dress-up dogfights. And it is a disservice because, like all pieces of arrant nonsense, it tempts sensible people to give a wide berth to the subject it has barged in upon.

But it is precisely sensible people that cookery needs—people whose only criterion for food is whether, on balance, it is delectable. The question is not whether it is plain or fancy, trendy or passé (people in New York restaurants this very noon will actually order mineral water because white wine, which last year was more in than martinis, is this year more out than flowered ties). The passion for labeling food, cooks, and restaurants as "gourmet" has done little more than give good food a bad name, bad food a good name, and every sane person a pain in the palate. For, in a world already full of dreadful divisions, it divides us further still. We become either antigourmets who won't touch anything but fried flounder, if that, or progourmets who hoke up every poor fish they touch. But the whole business is fishy in the worst sense of the word. So to begin your renewal, I shall once again go myself one better and give you nine sauces for pasta that are merely, supremely good. All but the last are made from canned fish. Let the trendsetters make what they want of that: for all they know, this could be the start of the canned-fish trend. In any case, we have better things to do with our time; and for the absolutely simplest of openers,

ANCHOVY BUTTER

☐ Cream together thoroughly with a spoon equal parts of soft butter and anchovy paste.

Mix into hot drained pasta and serve. ☐

WHITE ANCHOVY SAUCE

☐ Heat ½ cup olive oil and ¼ cup butter in a saucepan and simmer in it 5 anchovy fillets and a clove of garlic, all minced fine.

Cook until well blended (3 minutes or so), toss in a handful of chopped parsley, and serve over pasta. ☐

RED ANCHOVY SAUCE

☐ Chop fine a small can of anchovy fillets; chop up a dozen or so black olives and 3 T. capers; mince a clove of garlic.

Put a little olive oil in a saucepan, simmer the garlic for a bit, then add 1 cup Tomato Sauce (p. 107), a handful of chopped parsley, and the anchovies, olives, and capers. Simmer for 5 minutes more, thin with a little water if necessary, and serve over pasta. □

Incidentally, if your cleaver technique is improving according to schedule, there are two more jobs you can tackle with the *choy doh:* the mashing of anchovies, and the pitting of olives. For the first, simply treat the fillets as if they were cloves of garlic or slices of ginger: bring the flat of the cleaver down squarely on the little fellows. If your blow is out of parallel with the cutting board, of course, you will find your walls and backsplashes decorated with particles of anchovy to match the garlic bits that got there before them. But then, that's just an incentive to better technique which, in the meantime, makes your kitchen smell more orthodox.

As for the second, do the same thing: hit the olives one by one with the flat of the blade. The force required will be learned by practice; in any case it will be above the level of a love tap but below the degree of decisiveness which smashes the pits to pieces. After you have hit them all, just break away the loosened flesh of the olives and deal with them as your recipe requires. What do you do with the bits that still adhere to the stones? You put the stones in your mouth and enjoy an olive snack while you work—with, perhaps, a little glass of wine.

WHITE TUNA SAUCE

□ Drain a small can of tunafish and chop up the fish a bit; mince a clove of garlic.

Heat ¼ cup butter and ¼ cup olive oil in a saucepan and simmer the garlic until it is soft. Then add the tuna and simmer until everything is well blended.

Add black pepper, a handful of chopped parsley, and ¼ cup stock, bring to a boil, and serve over pasta. □

RED TUNA SAUCE

□ Slice ¼ lb. fresh mushrooms (or a small can of mushrooms), drain a small can of tuna and chop up the fish, and mince a clove of garlic.

Put a little olive oil in a saucepan, simmer the garlic in it awhile, then add the tuna and mushrooms and cook for a few minutes until well blended.

Add ½ cup Tomato Sauce (p. 107) and a handful of chopped parsley, boil for a minute, and serve over pasta. □

WHITE CLAM SAUCE

□ Open a can of minced clams, reserving the liquid (or steam open some fresh clams and grind yourself a comparable quantity); mince 3 cloves garlic.

Put ¼ cup butter and ¼ cup olive oil in a saucepan and simmer the garlic until soft and golden. Add the minced clams, ½ cup clam juice, ½ cup dry white wine, a handful of chopped parsley, and black pepper and oregano to taste.

Boil until the liquid is fairly well reduced and serve over pasta.   □

RED CLAM SAUCE

□ Make the sauce as above, but after it is reduced, add a cup of Tomato Sauce (p. 107), boil again, and serve.   □

If you ever have fresh, tiny hard clams you might want to try making your sauce this way:

WHOLE CLAM SAUCE WITH GARLIC

☐ Wash well 2 dozen small hard clams. Peel, but do not smash, 12 cloves garlic.

Put equal parts olive oil and butter in a pot big enough to hold all the clams, add the garlic cloves and let them simmer a bit without browning, then add white wine and let everything boil gently until the garlic is tender and the wine is nearly gone.

Put the clams in all at once, sprinkle with black pepper and oregano, cover, and steam until all the clams have opened.

Put hot drained pasta on a hot platter, arrange the clams, shells and all, tastefully on top, and pour the sauce with the garlic cloves and some chopped fresh parsley over all.   ☐

You wonder about the garlic? Don't. It's raw garlic that bedevils your breath. Cooked garlic is as harmless as cooked onion, and just as delicious. But since most people don't know that, you will probably be able to have them all to yourself, and get a reputation for bravery in the bargain.

SHRIMP SAUCE

☐ Shell and devein 1 lb. raw shrimp and simmer them in ¼ cup butter for 3 or 4 minutes; as they cook, add some tarragon, a little ground fennel, salt, and pepper, all to taste, and at the end, add a splash of cognac. Ignite it if you like, but you don't have to. In any case, cut up the shrimp a bit and reserve them.

Add some more butter to the saucepan, simmer a bruised clove of garlic in it awhile, discard the garlic, and add ½ cup Tomato Sauce (p. 107).

Bring to a boil, add the shrimp and a handful of chopped parsley, heat through without boiling again, and serve over pasta.   □

The shrimp in the last sauce—and the fresh clams in the one before it—bring us to the principle I want to commend to you for the period of your renewal. In essence, it is nothing more than an application to the creatures of the sea of the guidelines we have already used elsewhere: variety in the raw materials involved, and simplicity—or at least brevity —in the cooking methods employed. Accordingly, I am going to suggest that you cook as many different kinds of fish, fin- and shell-, as your circumstances will permit, and that you cook them all on top of the stove.

Unfortunately, this is one of the few advices in this book that literally has everything to do with the price of fish. And that, as you know, is ridiculous—or at least would be, if anyone were laughing. With decent shrimp at nearly $4.00 a pound and even squid at 57¢, what should be at least a twice-a-week ordinary meal is all too often a once-a-month special event. As with so many of the good, simple things of life, the market has made them first expensive and finally unavailable. At the turn of the century, workingmen had oyster stew for dinner; the last time I had it at home was years ago.

Clearly then, if you are going to cook more fish, you will have to develop a few stratagems to deal with this sad situation. The first one is to visit your fish market often, always buying the cheapest, freshest item you can find—and then worry about how you're going to cook it on the way home. Indeed, this is the one really frugal way to shop. The cook who goes out with a recipe already in mind may or may not be rich; but in any case, she is acting so, and paying accordingly. However, she is also limiting herself to what she already has in mind—a practice that, unless her mind is extremely well furnished, leaves her virtually closed to suggestion. And since suggestibility is the front door to that variety which is the spice of life, she is all too likely to end up in a tiresome alternation between flounder and shrimp till the end of her days.

The second stratagem is to make it known to your friends that you will take any kind of fish they care to unload on you. The world, mercifully, is still full of fishermen; and while they, like God and the market, are maddeningly undependable from a cook's point of view, they do, like God, come through at least from time to time with real largesse. Admittedly, they usually bring more than you want; thirty mackerel at a clip, a half-bushel grapefruit bag stuffed with blues, or a forty-pound striper laid out on your kitchen counter like a corpse. And invariably it is delivered at 6:30 P.M., when you are dressed to go out for dinner. In spite of all the inconveniences, though, you must never say no. Fishers, whether of fish or of men, see themselves as a put-upon lot. They spend so much time getting negative replies from nature and nature's God, that their tolerance for refusals from human beings is nil: even the slightest hesitation on your part will get you crossed off their list for good. Off with the jacket and vest then, and on with the old apron. Gut, fillet, wrap, and freeze until your counter is clear again. Besides, how many of those dinner parties ever started on time?

But it is the third stratagem to which you must pay the strictest attention if you are to improve the poor state of fish cookery among us: buy no precooked frozen seafood items at all. Fish frozen when it was fresh is perfectly all right— not quite the same as fish cooked right out of the water, to be sure, but more than good enough, and practically inevitable, given the nature of the fish supply, free or otherwise. But most of the thaw-heat-and-eat propositions are unmitigatedly and indescribably awful: breaded sticks of tasteless *Whatever*-fish (*Disgustosa blandiforma*), prefried shrimp with the texture of leather and the density of uranium, and little pouches full of Sauce Triste and scallop scraps. It is no proof of a cook that she can punch her way out of a plastic bag. Swear off the convenience foods, therefore—above all when it comes to fish. Given a minimum of good advice, anyone can do better from scratch at home.

On then with the advice. The first piece has already been given: cook your fish on top of the stove in a frying pan. The second is: cook it in butter or olive oil, nothing else. The third is: don't overcook it. I am always disconcerted by the times which most cookbooks give for cooking fish. Ten minutes for flounder is a crime; three or four is all it needs, if that. The main rule is that fish is done when the heat of cooking has changed the center of the thickest part from its raw, glistering translucency to a nice opacity. Anything more is just a merciless wringing out of the juices that make it the delectable creature it is.

You may, of course, literally *fry* your fish; that is, put a nice color on the outside in a hot pan (with or without coating it with seasoned flour, cornmeal, or crumbs beforehand). But remember that you may also *poach* it gently in bubbling butter as well. Use a moderate flame and a cover; it will be done in short order, and taste like nothing but its own fresh self. In fact, cooking fish by this method is the best way to learn what different fishes taste like. By and large, our usual division of fish into oily and nonoily ones is a disservice, particularly to the white kinds. We lump flounder, halibut, haddock, and cod together as if they were all the same thing. But they are not; and there is no better way to discover their uniquenesses than by poaching them plain in butter and serving them with nothing but some lemon wedges and a good boiled potato.

Nevertheless, whether you fry or poach, a little sauce never hurts, provided you keep it appropriately simple. For example, when your fish fillets or steaks have been sufficiently but briefly cooked, remove them to a warmed platter and look at the pan. Ask yourself: What does it need? If you fried your fish, there are bits of brown goodness that should find a better home than the drain in the kitchen sink; and if you poached it, the juices of the fish have already turned the butter into a sauce in its own right. Begin modestly, though: if the fish is nonoily, perhaps all you need is a little more butter and some lemon juice swirled in the pan with black pepper. Or a tablespoonful of capers with some of the vinegar from the jar. Or, if you want something more emphatic, try either of the above after blackening the butter (you don't actually blacken it, of course; only brown it nicely before adding the lemon juice or vinegar). Then too, there is always the possibility of a splash of white wine, boiled away till it is almost gone. In any case, a minute's extra care gives you a perfect butter sauce, and instant status as a cook.

If the fish is oily, you have more latitude: a little Tomato Sauce in the butter makes a nice addition, as does the merest hint of Worcestershire, or red pepper sauce, or both. And, of course, a little onion or garlic always helps an emphatic fish: simply mince it very fine and, after the fish is out of the pan, soften it briefly in extra butter before adding the tomato or whatever else comes to mind. You are a free agent. With even a little resourcefulness, you should be able to come up with a dozen finishes for fish based on nothing but butter and one minute's work.

Just in case you'd like something ever so slightly more elaborate, however, let me give you three more general advices. I shall couch them in terms of specific recipes, one for mackerel, one for bluefish, and the third for shrimp, but you will find the first two as serviceable for any oily fish as the last is for the generality of nonoily seafoods. Use them as you like.

MACKEREL IN DILL SAUCE

☐ Butter a cold skillet lightly; sprinkle some fillets of mackerel with salt, pepper, and chopped fresh dill (or dill weed) on both sides, put them in the pan and add boiling Court Bouillon, or fish stock, to the depth of the fillets. Add vinegar or lemon juice and more dill, all to taste, and simmer the fish, covered, till it is barely done.

Meanwhile, in a saucepan melt butter and blend in flour (use equal quantities: 2 T. each will thicken 1 cup liquid) to make a *roux*.

When the fish is done, carefully pour the liquid off the fillets, leaving them intact in the skillet. Measure out an appropriate amount of liquid, add it to the saucepan containing the *roux*, and, stirring constantly, boil it to the consistency of a nice sauce. Add a splash of heavy cream, correct the seasoning (salt? dill? vinegar?), pour it over the fillets in the pan, heat through once more, and serve with boiled potatoes. ☐

Court Bouillon, or fish stock? Simple.

COURT BOUILLON

☐ Put a quart of water in a pot, undersalt it, acidulate it with a little dry white wine (or lemon juice, or vinegar) and add some flavoring—a little chopped onion, carrot, celery, and parsley; a pinch of thyme, a blade of mace, some whole peppercorns, a bay leaf, and a small clove.

Boil for one minute, strain, and use for poaching fish, or as a base for sauces. ☐

Fish stock is the same thing with fish bones and trimmings added, and simmered for twenty to thirty minutes. Nonoily fish makes the best stock, but if all you've got is the racks of the mackerel you've just filleted, go ahead and use them. There is a Biblical injunction against seething a kid in its mother's milk, but none, to my knowledge, against poaching a fish with the juice of its own skeleton.

BLUEFISH, GREEK-STYLE

☐ Brush some fillets of bluefish or striped bass with olive oil, salt and pepper them, put them in a baking dish, and sprinkle them with a little oregano and some ouzo (or some other anise-flavored liquor).

Cut a large onion and a large tomato into very thin slices crosswise and lay the slices (alternating them) in overlapping fashion down the center of each fillet.

Season again with olive oil, salt, pepper, oregano, and ouzo and bake in a very hot oven (500°) until the fish is just done and the edges of the onion and tomato have begun to blacken. (If the latter doesn't happen, a quick pass under the broiler at the end will hurry it along without drying out the fish.)

Serve with anything, Greek or not.   ☐

SHRIMP IN GREEN SAUCE

☐ Shell and devein some decent-size raw shrimp; put some olive oil (or butter) in a skillet, heat it, toss in 2 peeled, bruised cloves of garlic, simmer briefly, and remove and reserve the garlic. Turn up the fire, add the shrimp. Throw on a splash of sherry, salt discreetly, cook briefly till they are curled and pink all over, and spoon them out of the pan into a bowl.

Mash the garlic in a mortar with a good palmful of chopped parsley, then add 2 T. flour, a pinch of ginger, and salt and pepper to taste; blend thoroughly.

Empty the contents of the mortar into the skillet, stir well over moderate heat, and add ½ cup dry white wine and ¼ cup water; cook until thickened, return the shrimp to the pan, add light cream (or milk) until the sauce is a good consistency, correct the seasoning, heat through. Serve with saffron rice if you're feeling not only very Spanish but very rich.   □

As I said, bluefish, albacore (horse mackerel), fresh tuna, etc., do very nicely by the first two recipes; and halibut, haddock, cod, and the like serve well in the last. But since we've brought up saffron rice (wash the rice as always, but before putting it in the pot, simmer some minced onion in olive oil, pound some saffron in a mortar with a little salt, add it to the onion, stir in the washed rice till it is all colored, add water sufficient, and cook as usual), let me give you something more opulently Spanish to go with it.

ZARZUELA DE MARISCOS
(SPANISH SEAFOOD CASSEROLE)

□ Shell and devein 1 lb. raw shrimp; cut 1 lb. halibut into chunks. Put some olive oil in the bottom of a large skillet with a little salt, get it very hot, toss in the halibut, and cook it briefly, letting it brown as it will but not letting it break up. Add the shrimp, cook it till it is just pink all over, and finally throw in a generous splash of cognac and ignite it; remove the fish and shrimp to a warm bowl.

Add more olive oil if necessary, and toss in 1 whole clove of garlic and a medium onion, minced; cook until soft and remove and reserve the garlic.

Add 2 tomatoes, peeled and chopped, to the pan, along with 1 pimiento, diced; mash the garlic in a mortar with a palmful of chopped parsley and put that in the pan; add $\frac{1}{2}$ cup dry white wine, $\frac{1}{4}$ cup finely grated blanched almonds, and bring to a boil.

Return the fish and shrimp to the pan, put 2 dozen scrubbed fresh mussels or small clams on top, cover, and steam gently until the bivalves open.

Correct the seasoning, and serve with saffron rice and peas.   □

In spite of the expense involved, let me end this chapter with a burst of shrimp dishes: the one that I still owe you—I've already given you the Shrimp Toast (p. 97) for the Chinese buffet—and two more for good measure.

PUFF SHRIMP

□ Prepare the shrimp: peel some good-size shrimp, leaving the tail section of the shell on, and devein them. With the point of a knife, cut each one lengthwise on the underside, but do not cut all the way through to the top. Smash a clove of garlic very fine, put it in a bowl with some lemon juice, toss the shrimp in the mixture, and arrange them tastefully on a platter; cover and chill till needed.

Make the batter: into a bowl sift 1½ cups flour, 1 T. baking powder, and ½ tsp. salt; add ½ cup peanut oil and stir the mixture to a dough; then add cold water and stir the dough to a batter that has the consistency of very heavy cream (1 cup water, more or less, should do it).

Heat oil for deep frying (if you have a butane table burner, put it on the buffet and let the guests dip and fry their own shrimp; if not, use the stove and do it for them). Dip the shrimp one by one in the batter, holding them by the tails, and put them into the deep oil till they are puffed and a good color; serve with an assortment of dips: soy sauce, hot mustard, hot sesame oil, white vinegar, oyster sauce, etc.   □

The next dish isn't quite what it seems: the phrase "with lobster sauce" doesn't mean there's lobster in the sauce—only that the recipe is classically used for lobster. It is, in fact, Lobster Cantonese made with shrimp. The egg, by the way, is stirred in only at the end, after the fire is off.

SHRIMP WITH LOBSTER SAUCE

☐ Mince 3 cloves garlic and 1 slice fresh ginger. Rinse and mince 3 T. Chinese salted black beans. Marinate (see p. 11) ½ lb. ground pork. Shell and devein 1 lb. raw shrimp; chop 1 scallion; beat 1 egg lightly. Have at hand peanut oil, salt, 1½ cups hot stock, and a thickening solution of cornstarch mixed with cold water.

Heat the wok very hot. Add a little peanut oil and salt, then add the garlic, ginger, and black bean, and stir-fry 20 seconds; add the ground pork and stir-fry for 1 minute; add the shrimp and the stock, cover, and boil 3 minutes; thicken judiciously with the cornstarch mixture, add the scallion, and turn the fire off (or remove the wok). Gently swirl in the beaten egg with a pair of chopsticks. Serve.   ☐

SHRIMP WITH KETCHUP SAUCE

☐ Mince 1 clove garlic and 1 slice fresh ginger. Shell and devein 1 lb. raw shrimp. Have at hand peanut oil, salt, sherry, ¼ cup hot stock, light soy sauce, ½ cup tomato catsup, and a thickening solution of cornstarch mixed with cold water.

Heat the wok very hot. Add a little peanut oil and salt, add the garlic and ginger, and stir-fry 10 seconds; add the shrimp and stir-fry 30 seconds; add a splash of sherry and the stock, and boil for 2 minutes; add 1 tsp. light soy and the tomato catsup, and boil. Thicken with the cornstarch mixture, then serve.   ☐

Once again, I have ended with a sure-fire favorite, and one using the great American taste-coverupper at that. In this case, however, it enhances rather than suppresses the shrimp—probably because, for all its popularity among us, it isn't really ours at all. *Ketchup* is Chinese for "tomato flavor." Tell that to the french-fry-drowning chauvinists in your house.

XIV

ENDING AT THE BEGINNING

e could, of course, go on and on. There are so many good things in the world, and so many dishes to be made from them, that I suppose it would be possible to cook lunch and dinner for a lifetime and never repeat yourself. Seriously. The longer I live, the more I think the major sin is boredom. Not blasphemy, which is just making proud noises when you can't think of anything better to do; not even idolatry, because that's only a silly escape from the real to the artificial. The true menace to life—the root of all the dangerous things we do—is being sick and tired. Wisdom is a firm resolve to be fed up with nothing except being fed up.

That is why this book, even though it contains more recipes than I first thought it would, is ultimately not a cookbook but a manual of renewal. If your appetite is whetted and your interest in certain dishes aroused, well and good; all real reform has to start somewhere. But the heart of the matter remains your own heart: getting it in the right place, and above all keeping it there—making sure it is permanently broken of its habit of loving the new prisons it so regularly builds the minute you turn your back on an old one.

For we are fonder of unfreedom than we think. Oh, we break our share of patterns—some of us more than others;

but few of us manage to break the pattern of imposing patterns, and none of us does it easily. Old Ernest galvanizes everyone to attention by breaking out and actually marrying Mrs. Loud. But the rate of recidivism is high: unless he kicks the habit of pouting and fuming until he's cornered her into doing things his way, he'll be back in the slammer in no time. Like the cook who goes shopping with a single recipe in mind, he removes the risk of being surprised by reality by deciding in advance what he will admit as real. And like her, if he insists upon his recipe at all costs, he will end up once again spending more and getting less—and wondering sadly how all his newness turned so quickly old.

It is not, you see, that we don't get bright ideas; it's that we take so long to learn that even the best idea cannot safely be turned into a universal principle. Things and people are at their best only when they are taken as surprises, by surprise. We learned that lesson well enough when we were little and loved the rabbit out of the hat without a single thought about housebreaking him into a possession. But that may have been because when we were children, we were closer to the great-grandfather of all surprises: the act by which we came into being out of nothing. In any event, when we are big, we tend to forget our magical condition. Having got used to being, we take it for granted—a gross error, because being has never been deeded over to us. It is only *being given* out of nothing, moment by moment.

The result is that we live our lives in fear. Silly fear to be sure: fear of the nothing that is the only thing God needs to make us be; fear that we will not be able to hold onto what we never had a firm grip on anyway. But fear nonetheless, and anger as well. We fret, for example, about whether there's life after death; we get the shakes at the thought that we will have to stop being after we've been. That's odd though: we've been nothing before. Why do we find it undisturbing to entertain the impossible and think about becoming a child again—to move backward, as it were, toward nothing—but tremble at the inevitable prospect of moving forward to it in death? Why berate God because we won't be around in 2078, yet spend not a minute getting worked up over the fact that we weren't here in 1878?

Well, because we forget that all our lives we have been up to our eyebrows in nothing. Annihilation is not the surprise: life is. Nothing is the water in which existence swims; it's a poor fish who spends his life complaining about being wet. Our frantic habit of toweling and powdering people so that they'll be dry enough for our taste is not only an exercise in futility, it's a missing of the very source of surprise. Your lifelong search for an antiperspirant against that cosmic wetness is a closing of your mind's eye to the most obvious thing about you: the fact that right now—in the only time ever really given at all—you are soaked to the skin in that nothing out of which, with a great splash, you leap home to him who made you.

Which is why resurrection, while it is a surprise like everything else, is not a bigger surprise. And above all, it certainly isn't anything new—let alone anything you have to impose some tricky pattern to achieve. In the Gospel, Jesus says *all* the dead are raised, the just and the unjust, the persuaded, and the unpersuaded, no matter what their persuasion. Like birth, resurrection is a universal fact, not an earned condition; and as with life, it requires only that you be sufficiently relaxed about nothingness so that you don't give yourself a hard time about *being* when it happens. Just be a good corpse; the rest was never up to you anyway.

No more heaviness then. Your beginning, as it always was, is in your end: it is quite safe to take yourself lightly. And, as a sacrament of that lightness, let me give you something elegant for dessert.

FOOD FOR THOUGHT   226

SALZBURGER NOCKERLN

☐ In a pie plate (or, better yet, a medium-size oval au gratin dish, if you have one) put 3 T. sweet butter, 2 T. milk, and 1 T. sugar.

Heat the oven to 450°, or higher, and put the dish in it while you beat the eggs.

Beat together 3 egg yolks, 5 T. sugar, 1 tsp. flour, and 1 tsp. grated lemon rind.

Beat 6 egg whites, with a pinch of salt and cream of tartar, until they form stiff peaks.

Lighten the yolk mixture by stirring into it some of the beaten white, and then carefully fold in the rest of the white, keeping the whole as light as possible.

Make a scoop, or shovel, out of several layers of 8½ × 11-in. stiff paper, freezer paper, or oak tag, take the dish out of the oven, and, using the shovel, scoop all of the mixture into the dish in 4 (four) giant blobs: the result should look like four huge dumplings in the dish.

Return the dish to the oven and bake at 450° for 6 minutes.

Remove, sprinkle with powdered sugar, and serve immediately.   ☐

Or, for the element of surprise to which lightness is the key, you might try instead

OMELETTE NORVEGIENNE

☐ With your hands, mold some good bulk vanilla ice cream (or another suitable flavor of your choice) into a billet, sausage, or mound that will sit fairly low in whatever freezer-to-oven dish you propose to use. Put it in the dish and let it all get thoroughly frigid in the freezer for 4 hours or so.

When you are ready, heat the oven to 450° or higher, and prepare the eggs as for Salzburger Nockerln above, using 6 whites but only 2 yolks.

Take the ice cream dish out of the freezer, and cover the ice cream with a thick layer of the egg mixture.

Put the rest of the mixture into a pastry bag fitted with a star tube and quickly pipe it onto the omelette in fleur-de-lis, kisses, or whatever strikes your fancy (alternatively, spoon it on so that it makes lots of peaks and swirls).

Put it right into the oven, give it 6 minutes, sprinkle with powdered sugar, and serve immediately.   □

There. You have established a working relationship with next to nothing; if you will now try your best to go the whole way and live by what you have begun to learn in cookery, it's all joy from here on out. Your best thoughts have always been things you never thought of before; your best relationships, the ones in which you got your sense of yourself sufficiently out of the way to be taken by the surprise of someone else. Openness is the key to the house with many mansions. Let go. You don't need to save fragments to shore against your ruin: you need to give them away. Elijah made the cruse of oil and the barrel of flour sufficient only after the widow of Zarephath finally used up all that was left. Jesus fed five thousand only after somebody gave away his fish sandwiches. In the kingdom, the best wine comes last— when all you ever thought was wine is gone.

So with Lazarus—and Ernest, me, and you. The party has always been in the works; it's only our insistence on trying to save it for a rainy day that keeps us eating soggy stuff. The world is a cosmic soufflé, and the last direction for enjoying any part of it is always the same: serve immediately and eat it all; there's another universe coming out of the oven in a minute.

Carbonara (for pasta) , 170–71
Carcass, chicken, fried, 94
Celery, beef with, 179
Charlotte, hot apple, 161–62
Cheese, in asparagus omelet, 114–15
Chicken
 and Peanuts (Kung Po Gai) , 61
 and rice (Gai Fun) , 46–47
 and rice stew (Asopao) , 140
 boned (sample dishes) , 167
 bones, sweet and sour, 94
 boning of, 92–93
 Congee, 137
 cutting up, 92–94
 diced, with almonds, 204–5
 flattened, 174–75
 Giblet Sauce, 173
 hacked, 196–97
 spatchcocked, with red sauce, 42
 steamed, 200
 wings, red-cooked, 189
 with almonds, 204–5
 with Asparagus (Revisited) , 53
 with Brown Bean Sauce, 203–4
Chicken livers
 red-cooked, 190
 sauce for pasta, 173
Chicken Skin and Cucumber Salad,
 197–98
Chickpeas, sautéed, 129
Chili, 187
Chili Powder, 187
Chinese Buffet, 193–98
Chinese cold noodle salad (Cold Lo
 Mein) , 195
Chinese Curry, 198–99
Chinese Roast Pork, 194–95
Chorizo, 186
Choy doh (Chinese cleaver) , 90–94
Clam sauce
 red, 211
 white, 211
 whole, with garlic, 212
Clams and Rice, 135–36
Cleaver, Chinese, 90–94
Cold Cucumber Salad, 120
Cold Lo Mein (Chinese cold noodle
 salad) , 195
Congee
 basic recipe, 136–37
 beef, 137
 chicken, 137

fish, 138
 pork, 139–40
Cornmeal
 mush, fried (Polenta) , 132–33
 Scrapple, 146
Court Bouillon, 217
Cream, clotted (Khaimak) , 161
Cucumber salad, cold, 120
Cucumber salad, chicken skin and,
 197–98
Curry, Chinese, 198–99
Cutting up a whole chicken, 92–94

Desserts
 bread pastry (Ekmek Khadayeef) ,
 161
 Hot Apple Charlotte, 161–62
 Omelette Norvegienne, 226–27
 Salzburger Nockerln, 226
 variations on Fondue Celestine,
 159–60
Diced Chicken with Almonds, 204–5
Dry-fried String Beans, 116

Eggplant
 casserole (Imam Bayeldi) , 45
 Szechwan braised, 117
Eggplant Sauce (for pasta) , 109
Eggs
 Asparagus-Cheese Omelet, 114–15
 Carbonara, 170–71
 Fondue Celestine, 158–60
 Moo Shee Pork, 202–3
 Omelette Norvegienne, 226–27
 Salzburger Nockerln, 226
 with onions, peppers, tomatoes
 (Piperade) , 116–17
Ekmek Khadayeef (bread pastry) ,
 160–61

Fish
 Bluefish, Greek-style, 218
 Congee, 138
 Mackerel in Dill Sauce, 216–17
 Shrimp in Green Sauce, 218–19
 steamed, 84–85
 sweet and sour, 94
 Zarzuela de Mariscos, 219–20
Fish sauces (for pasta) , 209–13
Flattened chicken, procedure, 174–75
Fondue Celestine, 158–60
 dessert variations on, 159–60

Fork, toasting (how to make), 100–101
Fried Potatoes, Greek-Style, 115–16
Fried Rice, 141–42

Gai Fun, 46–47
Garbanzos Salteados, 129
Gazpacho, 157–58
Giblet Sauce (for pasta), 173
Greek-style
  bluefish, 218
  fried potatoes, 115–16
Green Pepper Sauce (for pasta), 108–9
Greens, Barley, and Beans, 118–19

Hacked Chicken, 196–97
Ham Sauce (for pasta), 171
Hamburgers à la Steak Tartare, 176
Hot Apple Charlotte, 161–62

Imam Bayeldi, 45

Khaimak (clotted cream), 161
Knives
  Chinese cleaver (choy doh), 90–91
  general advice, 87–94
  sharpening, 89
Kung Po Gai, 61

Lamb, red-cooked, 190
Lettuce, with peas, 117–18
Lo Mein, cold (Chinese noodle salad), 195

Mackerel in Dill Sauce, 216–17
Meat loaf, steamed, 177–78
Meat sauce, plain (for pasta), 170
Meat sauces (for pasta), 169–73
Moo Shee Pork, 202–3
Moros y Cristianos, 130
Mushroom Sauce (for pasta), 108

Noodles
  Chinese Cold Noodle Salad (Lo Mein), 195
  three-flavor (Sam Jup Mein), 199

Omelet, asparagus-cheese, 114–15
Omelette Norvegienne, 226–27
Oyster sauce, and pork, 201

Paris Snacks, 176–77
Parsley Sauce, 107
Pasta
  Chinese Cold Noodle Salad (Lo Mein), 195
  fish sauces for, 209–13
  meat sauces for, 169–73
  Three-Flavor Noodles (Sam Jup Mein), 199
  vegetable sauces for, 105–10
Peanuts, and chicken (Kung Po Gai), 61
Pearl Balls, 177
Peas with Lettuce, 117–18
Pesto Genovese, 108
Pickled mustard cabbage (or sauerkraut), and pork, 201–2
Pilaf, 143
Piperade, 116–17
Polenta, 132–33
Pork
  and Oyster Sauce, 201
  and Pickled Mustard Cabbage (or Sauerkraut), 201–2
  and Samp (or Barley), 144
  and vegetables with eggs (Moo Shee Pork), 202
  boned (sample dishes), 167–68
  Chorizo, 186
  Congee, 139–40
  ground (Pearl Balls), 177
  Ham Sauce (for pasta), 171
  Moo Shee, 202–3
  roast, Chinese, 194–95
  Sausage and Rice, 134–35
  sausage, breakfast, 185–86
  sausage sauce, 172
  Scrapple, 146
  spare ribs
    barbecued, 196
    steamed, with black bean, 200
    sweet and sour, 94
Pot roast, Chinese (red-cooked beef), 191
Pot roast, royal, 45–46
Potatoes, fried, Greek-style, 115–16
Pots and pans, general advice, 80–84
Puff Shrimp, 220

Red Anchovy Sauce (for pasta), 209–10
Red Clam Sauce (for pasta), 211